Praise for *Healing Lazarus*

"Compelling. . . . [Richmond's] story's strength lies in the depiction of the arduousness and pain of recovery."
—*Library Journal*

"A moving, heart-opening, and gripping account of life taken and regained."
—Daniel Goleman, author of *Emotional Intelligence*

"[B]reathtaking, remarkably revealing, astonishingly articulate."
—Sylvia Boorstein, author of *It's Easier Than You Think*

"With unsparing honesty, Lewis Richmond unbuttons his humanity, and our humanity as well."
—Robert Aitken, author of *Taking the Path of Zen*

"I am so grateful that [Richmond] . . . had the courage to turn [his] experience into a profound teaching for the rest of us. This is an important book."
—Peter Coyote, actor and author of *Sleeping Where I Fall*

"Lewis Richmond uses the remarkable awareness of a highly trained Zen practitioner to give us an intimate account . . . [that is] outstanding in its sensitivity and depth of reflection."
—Roger Walsh, M.D., Ph.D., and author of *Essential Spirituality*

ALSO BY LEWIS RICHMOND

*Work as a Spiritual Practice: A Practical Buddhist
Approach to Inner Growth and Satisfaction on the Job*

HEALING
LAZARUS

A BUDDHIST'S JOURNEY FROM
NEAR DEATH TO NEW LIFE

LEWIS RICHMOND

ATRIA BOOKS

NEW YORK LONDON TORONTO SYDNEY SINGAPORE

ATRIA BOOKS

1230 Avenue of the Americas
New York, NY 10020

ISBN: 0-7434-2260-0
        0-7434-2261-9 (Pbk)

First Atria Books trade paperback edition October 2003

10   9   8   7   6   5   4   3   2   1

ATRIA BOOKS is a trademark of Simon & Schuster, Inc.

Manufactured in the United States of America

For information regarding special discounts for bulk purchases,
please contact Simon & Schuster Special Sales at 1-800-456-6798 or
business@simonandschuster.com

This book is dedicated to all those who are struggling with major illness, or suffering from physical or mental pain. May you be free from danger. May you have physical and mental happiness. May you enjoy peace and well-being.

CONTENTS

ACKNOWLEDGMENTS

In most books, the purpose of the acknowledgment section is to thank those who helped the author write the book. Here, its primary purpose is to thank those who saved my life. In fact, one might say that this entire book is one long acknowledgment. In the writing of the book I often used pseudonyms, in deference to peoples' wishes for privacy, but here it is my privilege to use real names.

To begin, a heartful thanks to all my doctors and healers: Dr. Robert Belknap, my family physician of twenty-five years, gifted diagnostician and good friend; Dr. Deborah Doherty, with her magic touch in treating the neurologically-impaired; Dr. Diane Englemann, a true listening woman; Dr. Arthur C. Fenn, the surgeon who opened my throat so I could breathe; Dr. Steven Frankel, whose warmth comforted me in my grief; Drs. Mary Ellen Guroy and Frederick Drach, infectious disease specialists and investigators *extraordinaire;* Dr. Barry Grundland; Lonner Holden, whose warm hands had such healing grace; Dr. Alan Margolin, chief physician during my stay in intensive care; Dr. Richard McAuliffe, who surgically implanted a feeding tube into my stomach that kept me alive for several weeks; Dr. Richard Mendius and Dr. Tracy Newkirk, both skillful and intuitive physicians; Dr. Paul Pelaquin, who offered me much-needed encouragement; The Ven. Segyu Rinpoche, who summoned my soul back from darkness; E.R. physicians Drs. Ray Brindley and William Teufel; Dr. Nancy Van Couvering, who was a pure comfort to me; and Dr. Peter Walsh, who most skillfully guided me back from the brink of darkness and despair.

Amy tried to keep a list of all my nurses' names as I passed through the various medical wards. I know we didn't get all of them, but thanks to Alex for his fearless spirit; Anarie for her steady hands; Charlotte for her kindness; Duncan for his great good spirits; Elvia for her stoic strength; Glenn for his patience and skill; Ingrid for her optimism and warm heart; Jill and Joan for their quiet excellence, and Jodie for her infectious good cheer; Kaija for her wealth of philosophy; Manny for his songs; Maria, Marcy, Martel, and Nympha for keeping the night demons at bay; Pat, Richard, Darryl, and Sally for calm in the face of chaos; Rhonda for her smile; Tim and Tom for their impressive expertise; and W.D. for his jokes. And to all the others who took such good care of me whose names I did not know or remember, thanks for your care and kindness.

I would like to offer a special thanks to all my physical therapists, especially Kathleen, Kristie, Laurie, Natalie, Sterling, and Wynne. During my long initial rehabilitation, they did so much of the hard work and heavy lifting.

Among the multitude of friends and family who rallied to my side, I would like to mention my sister Anna who sang me our childhood songs, Palden Alioto, Reb Anderson, Sylvia Boorstein, David Chadwick, Surya Das, Andy Dudnick, Matt and Jeannine Herron, Jack Kornfield, Yvonne Rand, Jay and Diane Rizzetto, Roger Walsh, Ken and Elizabeth Sawyer, Mel Weitsman, as well as all the hundreds of people far and wide who kept me in their prayers.

A special note of thanks too to Alan Rothenberg and my son Ivan, both of whom donated their own blood to me when mine faltered; and to Sue Rothenberg, Joan Busby and Hildy Burness, who took such good care of Amy while she was trying to take care of me.

Many healing memoirs do not have good things to say about insurance companies, but mine will be an exception: thanks to Julie Karpela, my case manager at the Principal Financial Group, for her concern and constant support, and to the company itself, which paid some $300,000 in medical bills—all of them.

And finally, thanks to all those who helped me produce this book: my agent Eileen Cope, my editor Tracy Behar, her associate Brenda Copeland and all the staff at Pocket Books, and Ben Yalom for his valuable editorial assistance.

I will say it again: this whole book is one long acknowledgment and warm embrace for all those people, named and unnamed, seen and unseen, who saw me through this time of darkness with their care, hard work, and love.

Thank you all.

INTRODUCTION

This story is the saga of a man who was nearly given up for dead, but who emerged from deep coma to embark on more than a year of difficult healing and eventual recovery. But it is also a story of the relationship of death to life, and life to death, and all the way stations between. As a former Buddhist priest and author, I tend to see this terrain with Buddhist eyes and will often describe it so, especially since this illness deepened my Buddhist understanding by making starkly real what was once somewhat theoretical. The first of Buddhism's Four Noble Truths—that suffering is an inevitable part of human life—is not so hard to under-stand intellectually, but when the suffering is yours, and goes on, week after week and month after month, it is not mere understanding, it becomes an authentic truth.

This illness also taught me that I could not rely on Buddhism for everything. Buddhism is based on having a clear, attentive mind, and the viral encephalitis that nearly took my life damaged my mind's clarity for several months. To heal I had to reach beyond everything I thought I knew and let the disease lead me and teach me. It was an often terrifying, sometimes amazing journey into the mysteries of the human mind—*my* mind. I am a different person now, and I hope a better one—more humble, more compassionate, aware that beneath the hustle and bustle of ordinary life lies a world of pain, courage, despair, and hope. As my doctor at the rehabilitation hospital said to me when I left, "You are one of the lucky ones." I left behind so many fellow patients whose minds and bodies would never be whole, who would struggle for months just to be able to lift an arm, or to say a word.

This long, difficult journey of healing also gradually revealed a hidden gift—the gradual opening of my heart. Before this illness, I was a quick-witted workaholic who coped with the crises of my life, such as my bout with cancer fifteen years before, by relying on my brainpower, energy, and problem-solving ability. During my year of chemotherapy and radiation I was for the most part cheerful and upbeat, and kept up a busy work schedule the whole time. But after the encephalitis I was a frightened, nearly helpless brain-damaged husk of my former self, dependent on my wife and the ministrations of my caregivers for nearly everything. The journey back, through fire and ice, forged a new person, one who could cry easily; my own suffering and that of my fellow patients gave me a renewed appreciation for the fragility and preciousness, as well as the resiliency, of life.

Nor do I feel that the journey I have taken is mine alone; the path of healing is universal. As I pondered what metaphor or myth might best express this universality, I consulted my knowledge of Buddhist scripture, but found myself instead drawn to the biblical Lazarus, the man who was raised from the dead. Although his story is one of the most famous in scripture, it is no more than a brief interlude in the Gospel of John. Mary of Bethany informs Jesus that her brother Lazarus is recently deceased, and begs Jesus to bring him back to life. Jesus does not hesitate. He accompanies Mary to the tomb, enters, and cries, "Lazarus, come forth!" And the Bible says, "He that was dead came forth."

That is all the scripture tells us of this extraordinary event. We do know that even for Jesus this was no easy feat; the scripture mentions twice that before he entered the tomb Jesus was "groaning," as though gathering within himself a great spiritual force. Most readers of this story may concentrate their attention on Jesus' extraordinary powers and their religious meaning. But what of Lazarus the man? Almost nothing is known of him. We don't know how old he was, or what trade he plied, or most importantly, what happened to him after he emerged from his tomb.

And how did he die? Was it from disease, or an accident, or old age? Was he struck down in violence? The Bible is silent regarding these details. And what was his condition when he was restored to life? Was he fully healed, or did he still suffer from illness, old age, or disability?

Our world is full of modern-day Lazaruses, people who have been rescued from certain death by medical miracles.

But these modern Lazaruses, though they survive, do not become young and perfect again. If they are old and infirm, they remain so; if the disease that would have killed them has disabled them, they remain disabled. It may be that Jesus' miracle was so extraordinary that the biblical Lazarus was restored to the prime of his life. Or he may have come back to life still weak and infirm. We do not know.

These gaps in Lazarus's story invite us to speculate, which in the service of describing the journey of healing I have presumed to do. Though we are not told his age, I imagine him as an elder, someone whose wisdom commanded great respect in his community. I wonder, could that be one of the reasons why Jesus agreed to lift him out of the grave? Is it possible that he intended to leave Lazarus in a confused, imperfect condition, so that he would have to make the slow, difficult journey from death to life, and be able to pass along what he learned to others?

To carry this speculation further, how would the members of his community have responded to this miracle? At first, of course, they would have been overjoyed. The great man Lazarus, whom they thought they had lost forever, had returned to the living. What a miracle! It would be only later that they would realize that Lazarus was not as he once was. He was confused, frightened, and mostly silent, but when he did speak it was of strange visions and a nameless terror from his time in the tomb. On occasion he would burst into tears or fly into rages for no apparent reason. He would ask, "Where is this place? Why am I here?"

His disciples—as an elder, I imagine he had disciples—would do their best to reassure him, but privately they would say among themselves, "This is not the teacher we once knew. His time in the tomb has altered him. He mind is like a child's, and he seems fearful of the simplest things."

What Lazarus and his disciples must discover is that the return from death, or near death, is not a sudden leap but a gradual journey. Whatever condition sent Lazarus to the tomb in the first place, he now has new wounds from the shock of being drawn so suddenly back into the light. Having spent four days in the death shroud, he doesn't have the words to express what he has experienced there, or to integrate it with his previous life. His family and disciples can only comfort the old man, hoping that soon—they don't know when—his confusion will clear and he will once again be the Lazarus that they remember.

Lazarus was brought forth by the touch of the hand of a miracle worker, who some said even then was the son of God. But now, his mind half light and half dark, Lazarus has to heal himself with no more divine help. His remembered wisdom will help him some, but not much. He is in new territory. Even his friends and disciples can do little more than comfort and support him. The hard work of healing can be shared, but not much; mostly it must be accomplished by him alone.

The reason why Lazarus serves as the theme and unifying thread of the book, and why each chapter begins with an imagined vignette from his new life, is not just because he is the hero of a famous story but because he represents all of us. Each of us has been, or someday could be, Lazarus. Each one of us could be a person who emerges from the tomb of our own serious illness, life crisis, or other catastrophe. When, sometime in our lives, we hear the command, "Lazarus, come forth!" we will understand that the person being spoken to is none other than ourselves. In their journey home, not everybody will follow in Lazarus's footsteps. But everyone will recognize the terrain—the steep cliffs, the sharp stones, the dense thickets, and all the other features that indicate we are feeling our way through the landscape of healing.

As for the real Lazarus, I imagine that in the goodness of time he emerged fully restored to his previous powers, but with a wisdom even greater than before, because he had a glimpse of human existence from both sides, emerging from the tomb like the newborn baby that we all once were and, deep within, still are.

ONE

STRUCK BY LIGHTNING

Lazarus, esteemed elder and learned scholar, walks down the central street of his hometown, scrolls under his arm, his robe pristine white, on his way to a study session with his students. As he passes, the town's inhabitants greet him by touching their hands to their foreheads in a sign of respect.

Suddenly, without warning, Lazarus stumbles, falls, and collapses senseless in the street. Immediately a crowd of people runs to his aid, and soon the news electrifies the entire town. Lazarus, the elder, has been struck down, as though by lightning, and even now is being borne to his home, while the town physician is urgently summoned.

What misfortune! What woe! the townspeople exclaim. What are we to do?

In Mill Valley, the suburb of San Francisco where I live, summer days are often cool and fog-shrouded. But July 1999 began with a heat wave. My family—my wife Amy and grown son Ivan—were looking forward to the July 4 weekend, a traditional time for us to barbecue hot dogs and corn on the cob, and later perhaps watch the fireworks at the local county fair.

After a busy week in my software business, I was not feeling well. On the day of the holiday, I was running a bit of a fever. But I felt well enough to participate in the festivities; I assumed I had a touch of the flu, or a summer cold.

Over the next week, however, the fever worsened. I was also beginning to feel a sharp pain between my eyes. I suspected a sinus infection, a chronic problem for me, and scheduled an appointment to see the nurse practitioner who assisted my regular family doctor. "Yes," she confirmed, after a quick examination, "looks like a sinus infection to me." She prescribed a sulfa drug and sent me home, certain that I would be well in a day or two.

I took the medicine, but the fever continued to climb. When it hit 103, I moved to the downstairs bedroom, where it was cooler, and began spending the whole day in bed. From then on my memory of events becomes vague. Amy tells me I spent three days in that bedroom, each day sicker than the last, taking powerful pain pills for my headache and sleeping much of each day. Finally, one evening I telephoned my physician's on-call doctor to report that I was beginning to have difficulty balancing, and had a roaring in my ears.

"Can you touch your chin to your neck?" he asked.

I could, but just barely.

"You'd better get down to the emergency room," he said. "Those are fairly striking symptoms. It could be meningitis."

"Go there now?" I said. It was already 9:00 P.M.

"Now," he said firmly.

I don't remember the trip. Amy told me later that I was so dizzy that the only way I could negotiate the outside stairs leading down to the garage was to sit down and slide backward, one step at a time. At the bottom I vomited. I do have a hazy memory of sitting in the car in the parking lot of the emergency room, my vertigo so severe I couldn't get out. When an aide had to lift me into a wheelchair, I cried out in pain.

I also remember the name of the emergency room doctor—Teufel, which I knew means "devil" in German.

"Teufel! The devil! I am in the hands of the devil!" I thought as they wheeled me into a stall on a gurney.

I have only a few further fragmentary memories of that evening before I lost consciousness—the voice and face of the kindly Doctor Teufel—in real life an angel, not devil—the roaring of the hospital fans, and Amy, hovering over me with loving concern. I also recall her face sometime later that evening, wrapped in a mask of metal foil. And I thought, "The devil's got her too!"

But there was a reason for the mask. Who knew what contagious horror I might be carrying? At this point the doctors could not be too careful.

I soon lost consciousness entirely.

For the next two weeks I would be a patient, not a person. It would be two weeks before I would emerge from deep coma and be lucid enough to understand what had happened—that I had been struck down by an acute and life-threatening case of viral encephalitis, a rare disease with various causes. Sometimes, as in the case of the West Nile virus that made headlines that same summer in New York, it is carried by mosquitoes, but this was not so in my case. The doctors suspected herpes zoster, the same virus that causes cold sores, but they could not prove it. In spite of the diligent efforts of several infectious disease specialists (they even sent a sample of my blood and spinal fluid to the Centers for Disease Control in Atlanta), no one was ever able to determine how one person in a suburb of San Francisco could come down with a disease more usually seen in Africa or Southeast Asia. My chances of getting it were probably about the same as being struck by lightning.

We read about random tragedies every day in the paper: a car full of joyous teenagers crashes, a kindly old woman is brutally murdered, a high school principal falls off a ladder while changing a lightbulb in his house and becomes a quadraplegic. We know these things happen all around us. They are a part of life, and yet most of us manage to avoid thinking about the possibility that they could be a part of *our* lives. Yet even today, nearly two years after the event, Amy and I still shake our heads in amazement at the shock, the suddenness and injustice of it all. Why did it have to happen to me? To us? Our lives had been going so well. I had recently published my first book, *Work as a Spiritual Practice,* which drew on my fifteen years as a Buddhist meditation teacher and another fifteen as a business entrepreneur. The business I founded was doing well; Amy had recently decided to leave her demanding job as a school principal for some well-deserved time off. I had just fulfilled a lifelong dream by releasing a commercial recording of original self-performed piano pieces. We were on top of the world. And then this!

In previous centuries life was not always so pleasant or secure. Then the lightning of personal tragedy struck regularly. Wars, famine, disease, poverty, all took their toll. Everyday life was an uncertain proposition. Ancient cultures sacrificed and prayed to their gods to spare them such suffering, and when it occurred, attributed it to the wrath of some offended deity.

And there were also ancient sages like the Buddha, who taught not of vengeful gods but of reason and wisdom. The study of Buddhism was my first career and occupied the first fifteen years of my adult life. As an ordained Zen Buddhist priest and meditation teacher, I taught classes and lectured, expounding the Buddha's ancient wisdom that life's woes were not the random whims of angry gods but the fundamental condition of human existence. "All human existence is characterized by duhkha," he taught, using a word often translated as "suffering," though the term has a deeper meaning that includes joy as well as sorrow, both of which are fleeting and unpredictable, bound to change and pass away. Though we may intellectually understand this truth, most of us tend not to dwell on it. Buddhist spiritual practice is designed to help us incorporate this truth into the way we live our lives. And though I expounded these teachings for years, and wrote about them in my first book, it was not until I suddenly found myself on a gurney in an emergency room, my last memory the face of my loving wife, that it hit me, like a clap of thunder, what the Buddha really meant.

Regardless of the place, regardless of how advanced and modern a civilization we have become, or how healthy and affluent, the tragic, unpredictable, and grievous lightning of suffering can strike at any time.

I had been a Buddhist for thirty years, and had the ordination certificates and teaching credentials to prove it, but I now feel that my true baptism into the Buddhist faith occurred on July 13, 1999, when the lightning of *dukkha* struck me down and my familiar, predictable, wonderful life of fifty-two years fell completely, disastrously, apart.

TWO

FEAR AND FIGHT

Lazarus lies motionless in his dark tomb, wrapped in a linen shroud. How did he come to be here? What cut short his ordinary life so suddenly? Outside, his wife, his friends and family, all comfort each other in their grief. Lazarus, just a few days ago so vibrant, so alive, is lost to them. Wherever he is now, it is not in their world. He is drifting in darkness.

Long ago in our evolutionary history, like all creatures human beings learned fear, in order to flee or fight. Whether it be some trivial apprehension or full-blown panic, we all know that fear is both unpleasant and, in its own primal way, often valuable.

Before this illness I was certainly familiar with fear in almost all its flavors and potencies, but the fear that I experienced as I sank into coma was of a different sort altogether. It manifested itself as a succession of extraordinary dreams, whose common theme was the urge to escape. Months later, I showed a transcript of these dreams to Dr. James, the psychiatrist treating me at that time. He agreed that they were unique, unlike any dreams of ordinary sleep. "Those dreams may be one reason why you survived," he said. "They kept your mind active, even in coma."

I am grateful for whatever forces constructed our brains to have such vivid and potent resources. These dreams may have been a direct expression of the all-out war between the encephalitis virus and my immune system. Who is to say how these mysterious connections between body and mind truly function? I will say this: in ten days, I dreamed a whole lifetime of vivid adventures, only a small fraction of which I include here. And though I have little memory of the days preceding my arrival in the emergency room, or what happened after, I still remember all these dreams after nearly two years. To the outside world, I was totally unconscious, but inside my head, I was active and aware, full of fear, fighting for my life.

As I arrived at the emergency room of Marin General Hospital, I was still conscious, but very confused. What was happening? What was wrong with me? Minute by minute I was losing my capacity to reason and my awareness of the outside world. Soon, and for the next ten days, the "real" world would be utterly lost to me. Everything I can now tell about what happened in that world, I learned later from Amy and others. Mine would be the world of coma, of darkness and the shroud. But strange to tell, it was not a blank world, not empty or silent. As mentioned above, I lived a lifetime of adventures there, in an never-ending sequence of brilliant dreams that had their own internal logic and a common goal—to escape. In this chapter and the next, I will write of these two worlds in alternation, sometimes describing mine, sometimes the "real" one. In fact they were both real, except that mine existed only inside my own head.

Back in the emergency room, the doctors saw my descent into coma as a dire, life-threatening sign. They did an emergency CAT scan, as well as a spinal tap, a painful experience that my waning consciousness pictured as two plumbers sticking screwdrivers in my back. The spinal tap's result confirmed the doctors' worst fears. My spinal fluid was full of white cells, where there should be none. There was an infection in my brain. And the CAT scan showed that my brain stem, at the top of the spinal cord, was swollen. It wouldn't be until they did an MRI scan (which required me to be transported to another building, something they could not do that night) that they could confirm what they suspected—viral encephalitis—but they began treatment immediately. The doctors pumped me full of acyclovir, an antiviral drug, along with massive doses of cortisone to control the swelling in the brain. For now, that was all they could do.

Amy stayed with me until 2:30 A.M., when I was about to be transferred to the intensive care ward, and the doctors told her, "There's nothing more you can do for him now. You should go home and get some sleep."

The minute she got home, around 3:00 A.M., the phone rang. It was one of the doctors calling to confirm that I was safely installed in intensive care, and that I was going to be "intubated," i.e. have tubes inserted in my throat to help me breathe. He wanted to make sure that she was not shocked the next morning when she came in and saw me. She has always been grateful for that doctor's small act of kindness.

What was it was like to be in a coma? I know there are books that describe the near-death experience in terms of brilliant lights, rapid movement, or even visions of deities. In my case, if any deities visited, they did not leave their calling cards, and the only travel I remember was a dream that every evening I was transported to a space station for storage! But my mind was continuously active with its survival dreams. As soon as one dream ended, another began. Each of them were epic struggles. Fear, and its partner fight, were the driving engines behind these visions—fear of dying, and the fight to survive.

I am flat on my back, on bare wood, surrounded by squatting South American Indians. They are shamans, about to perform a ceremony for my benefit. Amy is here, somewhere behind me. We are in the top floor of a multistory ceremonial structure, in the holiest of the rooms. Before me in an alcove there is an elaborate altar, with carvings, abstract painted patterns, and bowls of water and food. One old man, his face ancient with wrinkles, rises and touches my forehead with a feather. The other figures begin a low, deep chanting, and the ceremony begins.

I know the purpose of the ceremony is to transform me into a bird, a sacred bird who will fly away and be free. The old man circles my body again and again, performing various ritual movements and gestures with his hands. He touches my heart, my forehead, my feet, and sprinkles water on my bare belly. In the background I hear the voices of two of my Buddhist friends, one of whom is a recognized expert on shamanism. They are apparently part of an invisible audience to the proceedings. "This is quite an authentic example of the bird ceremony, don't you think?" he says to the other in a matter-of-fact tone. "Yes, yes indeed, best I've ever seen," comes the reply. I am annoyed. Why don't they help me? I am trapped here, my present human form about to be dissolved. Roger, John! I try to call out to them, but I am mute. The ceremony continues, on and on for hours, as I lie there helpless, unable to move.

At last I understand—not through speech, since I cannot understand the Indians' tongue, but intuitively—that for the ceremony to be successful, I must stop breathing. But if I do that I will die! Nevertheless, I want the ceremony to succeed. I want to escape. So I do it. My breathing, which has gradually become slower and slower, now stops completely. I must be dead. But nothing happens. I do not become a bird. I do not fly away. I simply feel very quiet and calm.

The Indians in the circle all rise and begin to disband. Apparently I am still alive after all, and the ceremony, though complete, is unsuccessful. I have not become a bird. What is going to happen next? Why won't anyone talk to me? In the background, I hear the voices of my two Buddhist friends chatting as they depart with the rest. "That's the full traditional form," I hear Roger say, one academic to another. "You rarely see it nowadays."

Day after day I lay still in my hospital bed, surrounded by beeping machinery, profoundly unresponsive. My heart kept beating, and my chest rose and fell, but that was all. Amy had by now been told by the doctors that I might not survive. Dr. Belknap, our family doctor of more than twenty years, had called her at home one evening to break this news to her as gently as he could. "Amy, things don't look good. I think we're going to have to start changing our thinking," was how he put it.

One afternoon at the hospital she leaned over my motionless body and whispered, "If you need to go, my darling, it's all right." Though I had not moved in days, my head suddenly jerked from side to side: No! Then I was still. For a moment Amy thought I actually had awakened. But no, I was just as before, still in a coma, my eyes staring blankly into space.

From a Buddhist perspective, all fear boils down to the fear of dying, of change and loss, the ending of all that we love and cherish. How deep that fear is, and how strong! Even in coma, when the mind is all but gone, it persists and pushes on, in my case serving a vital function—to keep me alive. It is often said that Buddhism sees fear as a kind of ignorance, or delusion. But even our delusions have their purpose, their reason for being, their gifts. Mine did. Sometimes the purpose was mere comfort, encouraging me that all was not lost, that life would go on:

My son Ivan, though not a musician, forms his own rock band. The band creates their own, more trendy versions of my original piano compositions, and Ivan plays them for me. The music is strange, electronic, barely recognizable as mine. Nevertheless, I feel grateful that he has gone to all this trouble to cheer me up.

Ivan contacts Eileen, my literary agent, to discuss the

*commercial possibilities of this music, and negotiates a
deal for it to be distributed in Japan. Instantly it is
done, and my music is a huge hit there. Everyone in
Japan wants to hear "Richimon," which is the name I
have been given there, in live performance.*

*But they know Richimon is a Buddhist, and they
expect Richimon to be a minimalist, "Zen" musician,
notwithstanding the rock-style music that Ivan has
distributed there. I am supposed to sit motionlessly
before a zitherlike instrument with an air of
meditative detachment and only occasionally pluck a
string. This is the style that is currently wildly popular.*

*I protest to Eileen that I am not that kind of
musician, and do not play that kind of music. "Don't
worry," she says. "Just play the role. You'll be fine." But
there is some other reason why this plan seems
impractical. Oh, yes. Now I remember. I am ill and
unconscious. I can't go anywhere.*

*In spite of this, I let the plans for the concert tour
proceed. The amount of money involved is huge.
Perhaps I will recover in time and be able to bring off
this role as "Zen" musician after all. The dream fades.
All that remains is this Japanese version of my last
name: Richimon. It will appear again in other dreams.*

To keep my fever down, I was wrapped in a special ice-cold
blanket. To protect my corneas from damage as my eyes
rolled from side to side, the nurses covered my eyes with cotton balls and tape. So that my fingers would not curl up like

claws, they filled rubber gloves with water and pressed them into my grasp, though I kept pushing them away.

Poisonous creatures, like crabs, nestle themselves into my hands, attaching themselves with their pincers. Over and over I grapple with them, trying to extricate myself by clenching and unclenching my fingers. On a horse farm, the proprietress leads a horse out of a stable and encourages me to mount and ride, but I lift my hands, showing her the crabs still attached to them, as a mute explanation of why I cannot ride.

To prevent my foot muscles from permanent damage, Amy, advised by one of the doctors, secured a pair of Converse sneakers for my feet. They were too small, and pinched my toes, but I felt no pain. I felt nothing at all.

We lived in a cave, our small band of Stone Age men and women. Our village was just outside, but it had been overrun by another tribe, ancestral enemies. I was the leader, and I had to find a way to retake the village and reclaim what was rightfully ours. But for some reason we all had cotton balls over our eyes and could not see. We communicated only by hearing and touch. Nevertheless, we made plans. We were a proud people. The enemy would not prevail.

In its fight for survival, my mind decided that no one and nothing could be trusted. My final memories, of a hospital filled with doctors and nurses, were transformed by my unconscious into the only explanation for my condition it could fathom, one in which cause and effect were confused. The doctors, far from being my rescuers, must be the cause of my condition, and thus my enemies. The nurses were their henchmen. Other important people in my life—my family and friends—were spies, plotting against me. I was like a condemned prisoner in a dungeon, shaking the window bars to see if they are loose, scouting the floor for a sharp object to dig with, constantly looking for a way out.

As my coma grew deeper, the tubes inserted down my throat were no longer adequate, and posed some danger of infection. So the doctors performed an operation called a tracheostomy to insert a plastic breathing apparatus in my throat, and open a breathing hole just below my larynx. This would prevent me from choking on my own fluids. A tight plastic band around my neck kept the apparatus from becoming dislodged. Periodically the breathing hole would fill with fluid, I would begin to choke, and a nurse would have to suction out the hole.

I have pain, just below my Adam's apple. It is a wound, a gash, an open sore. And to make matters worse, there is a tight band around my throat, a noose drawn so tight that I am immobilized as well as mute. I am a prisoner, but of whom? From the conversations I hear around me, the truth gradually becomes clear. I have been captured by members of a secret cult, based in

England, whose ancient roots reach back to the Druids, and who worship certain birds. One bird in particular is their god-king, dignified and handsome in appearance, with the fierceness of a falcon but the gentle curves of a dove.

Though this bird has been extinct for centuries, generation after generation this cult has been trying, through alchemy and magic, to bring it back to life. And at last they have finally succeeded—with me. Somehow the gash in the throat was an important part of the procedure. I still have the physical form of a man, but in their magical, cultic world, I am also a bird, their god, and the leash around my neck is to keep me from escaping.

My creation has caused enormous excitement among the cult members. The head of their band is a hyperactive young man in his twenties with the spiked hair of a punk rocker. His youth and charisma have captivated the other members, and he has great plans. The ancient power of the cult will rise again, he says, and to announce their new triumph to the world he plans to exhibit me to the world on the London stage.

Immediately the scene shifts, and I am being driven around the London theater district in a taxicab, still tethered to my leash, listening to the cockney-accented patter of the driver as he points out landmarks and places of interest. My status as god-king makes me deserving of this preliminary tour. Perhaps I am even supposed to choose the theater for my debut. But I have no interest in this wild ride; I am confused, exhausted, despairing. How can I extricate myself?

On Sunday July 23—when my condition was worst and the doctors most pessimistic—Amy and my son Ivan visited Yvonne, a close family friend and an experienced Buddhist teacher. Yvonne had led many through the labyrinth of death and dying, and knew many prayers and meditations in the Tibetan tradition, some of which she taught to Amy and Ivan, but mostly they all just cried together, their thoughts focused on my fading body back at the hospital.

Some days earlier, Yvonne had put in a call to a neurologist whom she knew in San Diego. Now, though it was Sunday, while Amy and Ivan were still there, the phone rang and it was he. He was unfazed by the dire medical report. "Don't give up," he said immediately. "Don't let the doctors have the last word. The brain has miraculous powers to heal. He could come out of it." He suggested that Amy start speaking directly to my brain cells and taught Yvonne what she should say. "Deep inside the brain where new cells form, new cells please meditate," she was to intone in my presence over and over again.

As Amy and Ivan were driving back from Yvonne's, Ivan suggested that they visit the place where many years ago we three had buried the ashes of our favorite family dog. He and Amy went and stood over the spot, in a secluded grove shaded with tall, stately redwood trees. The dog's name had been Ryan. When I had cancer, years ago, Ryan never left my side, and month after month lay with me in bed as I rested from the chemotherapy. Strangely enough, when my chemotherapy was over and I became well, Ryan became ill. I took him to the vet and discovered that he had developed cancer in exactly the spot I had had mine. The vet showed me the X rays of Ryan's tumor. I lifted my shirt and showed him the scar on my belly, in exactly the same location as Ryan's. The veterinarian said nothing; this was a little too spooky for his Western medical mind. From then on we had always referred to Ryan as our Medicine Dog. He was a beautiful dog, and had been buried in a beautiful place. Amy and Ivan spent some time communing with Medicine Dog.

A week earlier Yvonne had arranged for The Ven. Segyu Rinpoche, a healer in the Tibetan tradition, to come to my hospital room and perform a traditional healing ceremony over my immobile body. Though born in South America as the son of a Western-trained physician, he himself had left medical school in favor of an alternate healing path. Since his visit to my hospital room, he had been praying for me every day. Now, the day after Amy and Ivan had visited Yvonne, while Amy and my sister Anna were waiting at the hospital elevator door to leave the intensive care ward for lunch, the doors slid open and there was Segyu Rinpoche. In her own journal of this time, Anna described what he did on this surprise visit:

Lama Segyu is an open, expressive, unpretentious, warmhearted person. All last week, during his prayers

for Lew he had felt an image of growing blackness at
the base of Lew's skull, and today knew he had to return
immediately. He sat down at Lew's bedside, moistened
cotton balls with prayer-consecrated water, and put
them on Lew's forehead, throat, and heart. Then he
began chanting healing verses from a red-clothed book,
occasionally changing the position of the cotton balls. He
massaged various places on Lew's body with his
fingertips, in a clockwise, circular motion, and then
flicked his hands away as though dispersing energy.

Finally he took out some small cymbals and clanged
them three times over different parts of Lew's body.
Then he left us with detailed instructions about how to
visualize the color blue at the heart, throat, and solar
plexus, changing to orange as it moved up to Lew's
head.

Later that afternoon I noticed a change in Lew's eyes.
They seemed more present, less blank.

"If you can hear me, Lew," I said, "blink your eyes."
And he blinked!

It was one of the greatest moments of my life.

The neurologist in San Diego was not the only one who
disagreed with my medical team's prognosis. Jalal, my
business partner and a computer programmer, had had an
earlier career as a surgeon, and when my illness struck, he
was on vacation in Colorado. As soon as he heard the
news, he called Amy and listened carefully to her report.
Of course he knew all about viral encephalitis and how

serious a disease it was. But after he had heard Amy's report, his response was, "Lewis will fight, he will live," he said. "He is strong."

As he drove back from Colorado to San Francisco, he called Amy every day for updates, but in spite of the continued bad news his opinion did not change. Much later, during my recuperation, I asked him why he was so sure. "The doctors in the hospital didn't know you," he said, "but I did. I knew you would fight. Where I learned to practice medicine [he is a native of Iran] knowing the patient is very important."

I am floating in a tank of water in the kitchen of an ocean-going cruiser. Bound up with thick twine, I turn and bob in the liquid. Sometimes my face is submerged and I cannot breathe. Just as I am about to lose consciousness, my body turns in the water and I can take a breath. All around me are bustling people in cook's uniforms. Some of them look Hawaiian or Asian. Occasionally one of them pokes me with a long fork.

All their actions indicate they are preparing to boil me like a chicken. I cry out to them that there has been a terrible mistake. I do not belong here. I am Lewis Richmond, from California. Finally I mention that I am a patient of Dr. Belknap, my family physician. Please call him, I plead. Please. He will explain.

This seems to get their attention. At last I am lifted out of the tank and released from my trussing. For patients of Dr. Belknap, they explain, there is a special

dispensation. On ocean liners everywhere, he has made
arrangements for his patients to be exempt from the
usual treatment. I am enormously relieved. At last I can
breathe normally.

Once, in the early days of the San Francisco Zen Center's
development of the Tassajara Zen monastery in the
Santa Lucia Mountains of California, Buddhist teacher
Shunryu Suzuki was enjoying the cool water of a swimming hole in the Tassajara creek. None of the students
with him knew that he did not know how to swim, and
when he disappeared from view for a few moments, it
took them a while to realize that he was underwater and
was not coming up. Several of the men jumped in and
pulled him out. He was gasping and choking, and had
almost drowned.

He talked about this incident in several subsequent lectures, how for the first time in decades, he had felt the fear
of death surge through his body. In his mind, a true Zen
master should have no fear of dying, and he humbly
admitted that he would now work harder on his own
Buddhist practice.

A few years later, when I read transcripts of these lectures (I was not present at the swimming hole), I was
greatly impressed by this story. No fear of death. The true
Zen spirit! But now, after thirty years, my attitude has
changed. Perhaps there may have been some extraordinary Buddhist adepts who were able, through long years
of meditation, to neutralize the fear of death, and the

fight to survive, that is programmed into every cell in our body. But for most of us that fear of death, and will to fight, is our ally in times of crisis, indeed our friend.

Looking back to my time in coma, I have come to appreciate fear as part of the embedded wisdom of the mind and body. Far beneath the thin stratum of our waking conscious mind, it protects us, looks out for us, and perhaps even loves us. Without it, I would not be writing these words, nor you reading them. Without it, we would not be the mysterious, complex creatures that we are, and the miracle of healing that began in the depths of my coma, and continues even today, would never have occurred.

THREE

SURRENDER

Lazarus, lost in the world beyond, struggles frantically to find his way back to the land of the living. But the maze that traps him is too vast, too complex. He writhes and struggles to free himself, but it is no use. At last he lies back, exhausted, and feels, for the first time, the presence of warmth and light. The light has no form, but it has a quality of care that eases his pain. Lazarus can fight no more. He sleeps, and surrenders to the light.

After ten days, to everyone's amazement and relief, I began to come out of it. The first signs were little tremors in my fingers that at first only Amy and the nurses could see. But soon the doctors made a more thorough examination, and confirmed that my reflexes and other autonomic responses were indeed returning, and I was rapidly becoming more responsive. My eyes, which had for ten days been closed or fixed in a blank, dead stare, began to come alive, although for a while I could make out only vague shapes. I still couldn't talk—the breathing hole in my throat prevented that—but I could move my hands and head, and wiggle all the parts of my body. That was a good sign. I wasn't paralyzed, as the doctors had feared I might be. And when Amy spoke to me, I could hear her and recognize her voice, and reach out to clasp her hand in mine.

But still, the emergence from darkness was slow and gradual. For several days I was still disoriented, as my mind lingered in the realm of coma.

I open my eyes and see two wall clocks, one above the other. Where am I? When I close one eye, the two clocks become one, but I can't read the numbers. I feel the soft support of pillows under my head. My arms brush against sheets. I move my right arm a little farther and bump up against a tube of cold polished steel. I try to turn my head to see what it is, but it is too painful. I reach up and feel my nose, my lips, my chin. My beard feels scraggly, half an inch too long. Can I move my legs? I can knock my knees together, and press my feet against the foot of the bed, but that is all.

My head roars with a noise like radio static. I have an image of a cinnamon stick thrust through one ear and out the other, twirling inside my brain. I exhale and feel the air rush out through a hole in my throat. The hole fills with fluid, and I begin to choke. After a while someone leans over me and inserts a plastic tube into the hole, making a sucking sound. I cough convulsively for a few panicky moments, unable to breathe. Why am I being tormented like this?

I imagine the vivid presence of patients in other beds—a white-haired old lady, a middle-aged Chinese man, a small boy. I wonder why they never move or talk to me. Sometimes it is Amy or Ivan who is in these other beds. The head of a black woman, her expression stern, glares down at me from high above.

I know who I am, but only the way one knows oneself in a dream. Amy is with me now, her hand in mine, smoothing my hair, caressing my hand, stroking my arms. I can turn my head just enough to see her face, or rather two faces, one above the other. She is talking to me, but I can't understand much of what she says. The words "brain stem" and "virus" stick in my mind. When she stops speaking, I motion with my hand, urging her

to continue. As long as I can hear her voice, the
confusion that fills my whole being eases.

Eventually I began to grasp the meaning of Amy's words. Acyclovir, cortisone—these were medicines, I knew, and I understood that I was still being given them. But my thinking was not logical. I thought, for example, that my condition must be a side effect of the medicines. I imagined that the comings and goings of the nurses could be controlled with the tilt of my head. Nor were my sense perceptions accurate. There were no other beds in the room, no other patients—I was just imagining things. The head of the black woman staring down at me from on high was in actuality a wall-mounted television set. My sense of identity was becoming stronger. I now knew that I had been asleep, and was now awake. But what had happened to me?

Finally the disorientation began to subside. I could see now that I was in a hospital bed, with nurses coming and going, changing my dressings or disinfecting my stomach tube. And for as many hours as it was allowed, Amy was there by my side. How I cherished her presence. Her face next to me was the only familiar, helpful shape in this strange world. Each night she would carefully explain that she had to leave, and the precise time when she would return, and I would nod, thinking I understood. But when morning came I could not remember what she had said, and I strained to read the clock on the wall, to guess how much longer I would have to wait. From the first light of

31

dawn I would look constantly through the glass that separated my room from the nurses' station, thinking that every passing figure must be she. And when at last, hours later, I heard her familiar footsteps in the room and the sound of her voice, I would lift my right hand and wave with relief.

It was several days before I was sufficiently lucid to put together the story of my illness that Amy had been repeating to me for days—I had been deathly ill, but I had survived, and was going to need many months of rehabilitation and healing to become whole again.

I absorbed this news with mixed feelings. On the one hand, the story made sense, and logically accounted for all the things I saw in my room—the bed, the monitors, the nurses, the tubes, my weakened condition. At the same time I missed my dreams and their promise of escape. I asked Amy to tell me the story again and again, and as she did, I sighed in resignation. I knew now that it was true, and it made me very sad.

I had survived, but I was stripped of all my skills and abilities, and as I lay in bed, barely able to move, I despaired at the loss of my capacities, which I feared might be permanent. I couldn't walk, eat, or even talk. The best I could manage was some kind of primitive sign language. The doctors were relieved; they said not to worry, Amy told me, I would recover in time. And I thought, Yes, these were the same ones who had said I would die, too. How much can I trust them?

But my deepest worry concerned my mental faculties. I

didn't know the condition of my mind. Was my ability to reason preserved? Would I ever be able to think and talk like a normal person, to manage my business again, to write other books, to compose and play music? I had always prided myself on being a smart, capable person. The possibility that my mind might be damaged was terrifying.

I once read of a great mathematician who was dying, and stayed up nights screaming because the cancer was destroying his world-class mind, and he was helpless in the face of it. Would it be like that for me? Yes, I had cheated death, but at what cost? Some part of me was still hoping to escape.

I dream. Amy is sitting by my bed. She apologetically explains that she has crashed our car. It happened when she found out about a secret meeting of the bird cult in the Nevada desert, and drove out there to plead with them to release me. There she discovered that the American branch of the cult operated under different leadership. Here the leader was a middle-aged woman, a British expatriate, who represented the "traditional" wing of the cult, following all the ancient rules to the letter. This woman was outraged that the English branch of the cult had performed the bird-god imprisonment ceremony on me. "It's totally against the rules to do such a thing without the express permission of the subject," she said. If it were up to her, she would have me released immediately, but the English branch had me in their possession, and I was beyond her reach.

After telling me this story, Amy apologized again about the car, but I dismissed her concerns. No problem, we'd just buy a new one. There was a car dealership, I knew, on the ground floor of the hospital. All she needed to do was arrange for me to be transported there, and we could drive away in a new car and escape from all our troubles.

Instantly I found myself in the elevator, going down. On the ground floor, I was met by a physician who performed a detoxification procedure to flush out all the medicines and drugs that were in my body. Then I was wheeled on my stretcher into the car showroom, where several nurses waved pine branches over my body and chanted Buddhist prayers. They all knew I was a Buddhist author, and had read my book.

Now I was seated in a sporty red convertible, listening to an effusive salesman tout its many features. But I could not open my eyes or raise my head up from the back of the seat cushion. I tried as hard as I could, and asked for their help, but it was no use. How was I going to drive if I could not see? Didn't the car have a feature that would allow me to do this?

Yes, said the salesman, it did. A young, fast-talking black youth appeared and showed me the special control next to the gearshift lever, a flexible plastic tube into which the driver inserted his hand. "It's no problem, man," he said, inserting his own hand and demonstrating the various movements required to control the car without having to see. "I can do all kinds of tricks with this baby. Here, try it." And he helped me insert my own hand into the tube so I could practice.

Now Amy was in the passenger seat. Should I let her do the driving? No, it was a matter of pride that I be able to do it. I kept practicing with my hand in the tube.

Mary, my business partner, now appeared. She had taken a job in the car dealership as a preparer of new cars. She bustled about the car with the same thoroughness and efficiency with which she functioned at work, polishing the windshield, checking the oil and transmission fluid. She also swabbed my mouth out with flavored cotton, as the nurses in the hospital did, combed my hair, and washed my face. I began to grow impatient. When could we drive away and go home?

At last the moment came. I started the car and lurched forward to the driveway and the street. But before I knew it, we were back on the sales floor. Some problem had come up.

In my dreams, some problem always came up. Whatever escape plan my dream had concocted would never come about. Even though I was now mostly conscious, I was still fighting, still struggling to find a way out. But, as I was close to discovering, the time to fight was coming to an end. The time to yield and surrender was at hand.

Ivan was my first visitor besides Amy. He stood at the foot of the bed where I could see him without having to turn my head. "Hi, Dad!" he said, trying to sound cheerful. Here he was, my boy, the one who had always counted on me as the strong one. And now it was just the reverse; I was the weak one, depending on him. He looked so strong, so mature, with his full black beard and dark, intelligent eyes. I was so proud of him. In my delirium, in my dreams, he had protected me, and now here he was, in the flesh.

Next to visit me was Jack, Buddhist teacher and close personal friend. Seeing him standing over me with his gentle, affectionate gaze was so uplifting. He greeted me with the classic Buddhist gesture, palms together, and I instinctively tried to reciprocate, but I was too weak—such a simple thing, and I could not do it. I started to cry.

Jack did not speak right away. He allowed my grief to flow, and was comfortable with the silence that hung between us, intuitively understanding that his silent presence would help me more than any speeches. When he finally did speak, he said, "Lew, I think you have come back to us because you have some important work to do." More tears ran down my cheeks when I heard him say that. In his calm, meditative presence, I could feel the fight beginning to leave my body and acceptance beginning to sink in.

But as Amy now explained to me, my few visitors were only a tiny visible portion of those making efforts on my behalf. Among our circle of friends, and throughout the wider Buddhist community, as soon as I became ill the word had gone out: Lew Richmond was dying. So many people around the country had been praying for me since. At

Buddhist centers in San Francisco, New York, Los Angeles, Hawaii, and many other places, special services and meditations were performed on my behalf. When my life seemed to be slipping away, all these people, most of whom didn't even know me, freely shared their strength and spirit.

Before this illness, I would never have characterized myself as a strong believer in prayer. But as I write this now, I feel differently. We are all connected in mind and body, in ways we cannot fully comprehend. I had a wonderful team of doctors, who performed brilliantly in my hour of need, but I also had a much larger group of caregivers, scattered all across the country, helping me less visibly though with equal dedication.

Had I fully comprehended the power and meaning of this resource, I might have been able to let go of my fear and my desperate need to fight somewhat sooner. But the moment came soon enough. It was while one of the nurses was adjusting the position of my body, to make me more comfortable, that the revelation hit me like a thunderbolt: I had nothing to fear any longer. All I had to do was lie here and do nothing, think nothing, be nothing, and let all these wonderful people, with their soothing voices and tender hands, take care of me. My whole body was flooded with a profound sense of relief.

My intellect, which had been struggling so hard to understand, to cope, and to maintain some semblance of control, surrendered itself to this new feeling. At last my fevered brain had some respite, as my heart, so long imprisoned by fear, began to open like the bud of a new flower.

By temperament I had always been impatient, active, and assertive, always looking for a way to solve a problem, though there were remarkable times in meditation when I was able to experience this same profound sense of letting go. Surrender, I was beginning to learn, was as critical a part of healing as fighting. The trick was to know when to fight, and when to let go. When I had cancer, fifteen years ago, many of my spiritual friends advised me to just accept my disease, to let be what will be. But I could not do it. I fought it tooth and nail. I would not give in. With every treatment, with every radiation dose, I battled my disease like the bitterest of enemies. And I won. I was cured. That was a time to fight.

But this time was different. This time, flat on my back, barely able to move, unable to speak, there was nothing more I could do. Perhaps my Buddhist meditation experience helped me remember how important it is to allow others to step in and hold us, support us, and allow us to accept whatever our fate will be. I surrendered to that feeling and basked in its warm glow, suddenly confident that Amy, and Ivan, and the nurses and doctors, and all my friends, would take care of me fully and completely.

I had studied Buddhism formally for fifteen years, and informally for another fifteen, but never had I received such a profound lesson.

On August 2, I was to be transferred from the intensive care unit of the hospital to another hospital, where my rehabilitation was to begin. I had been in intensive care for twenty days. Before I left, one of the doctors came in to replace the plastic apparatus in my throat. He took the extra time necessary to do the procedure so that I could, temporarily anyway, make a sound.

For many minutes he yanked and pulled at the contraption inside my throat. Then he said, "Say something."

Say something? I had not spoken in nearly three weeks. I hardly knew what to do, how to form the words. What should I say?

I said the first thing that popped into my mind. "Hi!" I said to Amy and the kindly doctor. "Hi!" That sound was like a heaven-sent trumpet: my own voice, tinny and cautious, and full of trepidation, but still undoubtedly mine.

"Hi!"

One word, but it was such a thrill after so many days of silence. Suddenly, with that "Hi," I felt a little less frightened. Amy was overjoyed too. I waved my thanks to the doctor. I was saying "Hi" to him, and to Amy, but also to my return to the world, and to life.

FOUR

GRIEF

As Lazarus's relatives bore him home on a litter, they reached up again and again to touch him, to assure themselves that he still had the warmth of living rather than the chill of the dead. Once home, Lazarus's large house became a place of celebration. As feast food was prepared and set out, friends and relatives arrived to embrace Lazarus, whom they thought they would never see again.

To Lazarus, all the commotion and noise was overwhelming. "Please," he said whenever anyone leaned close enough to listen. "Please let me have quiet. I do not know where I have been, or what is to become of me. All I feel is sadness, so much sadness."

We all have a rich vocabulary of emotions, some superficial, some so deep that they can scar the soul. Grief is perhaps the most powerful of them all. Once the shock of my predicament set in, I was overwhelmed with sadness over my lost identity and shattered sense of self. I struggled to understand why this was so. My rational mind could not comprehend why I should be so upset. Hadn't the doctors at Marin General said I would recover? I was soon to hear the chief physician at Kentfield Rehabilitation Hospital, an expert in neurological healing, confirm that my prognosis was indeed good. This should have been cause for rejoicing, not sadness.

During my year of cancer treatment, fifteen years before, though the chemotherapy and radiation treatments often made me ill, and there was a real chance that I might actually die, I had remained cheerful and optimistic. I had never grieved. Why, when my chances were so much better now, was I so distraught?

One answer came many months later, during a joint meeting with a neurologist and a psychiatrist. I asked them why my response to this disease was so different than how I dealt with cancer, and they both answered at the same time, "Because it's your brain."

My brain had changed. Since my descent into coma,

and subsequent awakening, the mature, capable adult I was before the illness had gone missing, and in its place, it seemed, was an inconsolably sad little boy. It was as though a sturdy ocean pier had collapsed and was now lying broken and submerged in the water. The person that I had been for fifty-two years—all my skills, accomplishments, and abilities—was gone. Once a pianist with formidable dexterity, I could now barely move my fingers or hold a pencil. I had no idea if I could still write or do computer programming. The extent and permanence of the damage was as yet unknown to me. Could the pier be rebuilt? Could there be a new, restored "me"? I had only my doctors' preliminary assessment to go on—hardly a match for how awful I felt physically and mentally. Meanwhile my present self, the one that still held all my memories of who I had once been, still needed to mourn.

And mourn I did. It was only much later that I came to realize that grief, far from being something to be ashamed of, can be a great teacher, though its lessons are often difficult to grasp, and in this regard I was, for perhaps the first time in my life, a slow learner.

As the month of July ended, I was still in intensive care, enjoying my opening to surrender and trust and the letting go of fear. For the first time since my illness began, I felt safe. My mind grew clearer, as each day I left further behind the inner struggles of dreamtime that had so exhausted me. All day I would be soothed by Amy's presence and the sound of her voice. At night, I would slip into a drug-induced stupor, when I often imagined my feet floating up to the ceiling, while my head and shoulders remained cradled in a cluster of fragrant flowers.

On August 2, 1999, two ambulance drivers, one tall and blond, the other shorter and dark-haired, arrived in my hospital room to transport me to Kentfield Rehabilitation Hospital—a ten-minute drive. I had been expecting them; Amy had been explaining to me for several days now about this upcoming event. I was excited by their arrival, since it meant I would be leaving this room of near death and going to a place where my healing could begin, but the prospect of being lifted and moved for the first time in weeks made me anxious. Amy tried to reassure me, while she explained to the drivers to be careful with my neck, which was still painful from the swelling in my brain. There was no room for her in the ambulance, so she had to rely on them to take good care of me while she followed in her own car. She explained to them how I communicated: one finger for yes, two fingers for no. "I got it," the blond man grinned. "One finger yes, two no. Right?" And he chuckled when I raised one finger. The two of them, working in tandem, moving me inch by inch, slowly transferred me from my bed to their gurney, as my heart pounded in my ears. Then rolled me out of the room and down the hall. I was on my way.

Down the elevator and out of the hospital into the parking lot. The light was so bright. I felt as though I had suddenly emerged into a badly overexposed photograph. As the men lifted me and rolled me into the back of the van, and my body jerked and swayed, a jolt of pain shot through my neck. I waved my arms frantically, signaling my distress. The tall blond attendant crouched next to me in the back of the van and took my hand, which I gripped tightly for the duration of the short ride. And then the same process occurred in reverse: they lifted me out, a bit more slowly this time, and rolled me through sliding glass doors down a wide, brightly lit hallway. As they pushed me along, all I could see was the acoustic tiles on the ceiling rushing by.

Wait, where was Amy? Then I saw her. She had just caught up to us. As we passed the reception desk, she leaned down and told me she would be stopping there briefly, and not to worry, she would be right with me. Straining to turn my head a bit, I could see nurses bustling by, a crowd of what seemed to be visitors, and a few patients in hospital gowns on canes or crutches. I also noticed that every wall we passed was lined with a solid row of wheelchairs.

Then we made a left turn and rolled through a doorway into a room. The ambulance technicians carefully lifted me up and slid me into my new bed in a tiny curtained space, in a room I was apparently to share with another patient. From the other side of the curtain, my roommate called out a greeting, but the blond man, ready to leave at the door with his now-empty gurney, answered him, "He can't talk." Then they were gone, and I was alone, except for my invisible and now silent roommate, to count the minutes until Amy's return.

I waited in limbo, hardly daring to breathe, until at last Amy pushed through the curtains around my bed and was with me again, explaining it all to me: the admissions procedure, the paperwork, and an initial examination that was to happen soon, when I would meet the doctor who would be my primary healer for the next seven weeks.

Right away she handed me my alphabet board, the one she had made during my last days in intensive care so I could begin to communicate. I was just beginning to try it; it was still difficult for me to see the letters or to raise my hand far enough to point to the top rows. But I was able to tap out the question—"Am I okay?"

"Yes," Amy said. "Yes. You're okay. Everything's okay. The doctor will be in soon. She wants to talk to me for a few minutes now, then we'll both come back, and you can meet her."

More slow time passing, more anxious waiting, but at last the curtains parted, and Amy reappeared, along with a slender, attractive woman with long black hair, dressed in a white coat, holding a clipboard, and another older woman dressed in a floral smock, her face already beaming.

The younger woman took my hand in hers and shook it. "Hello. I'm Dr. Doherty, and this is Greta, one of our senior nurses."

Greta made a little bow. "How do you do, sir?" she said, her voice radiating warmth, her accent distinctively Scandinavian.

"How are you feeling?" the doctor asked.

How indeed? I made a little wiggle of my hand.

"Not so well, right?" She consulted her clipboard. "Viral encephalitis. You're a lucky man."

I reached for my alphabet board and spelled out, "I K-N-O-W, " as she leaned over, watching me.

In spite of my awkwardness in trying to point to the letters, she had no trouble following my finger. "You know, then, how lucky you are. You went into a coma awfully fast. They weren't sure if you were going to come out. Now I'm going to do an initial exam, to find out what you can do, and then Greta will draw some blood for some tests. Okay?"

I nodded. I liked this doctor. She was bright, efficient, and enthusiastic, and when she spoke to me I felt her total, undivided attention, a quality of hers I came to treasure as I got to know her better. The hospital's chief physician, she was always on the go, but whenever she was with me she always managed to make me feel I was her only patient.

The exam began. "Squeeze my hand," she instructed. "As hard as you can."

I did as she asked. "Wow!" she exclaimed, extricating herself from my grip. "You're strong." From a lifetime of piano playing I had unusually strong hands. Apparently even in my debilitated state they were still stronger than she expected.

"Lift your right arm, as high as you can."

I strained mightily and managed to lift it about four inches off the bed.

"Good." She paused and stepped back. "Now before we

go on, I'm going to tell you the name of four flowers, and in about ten minutes I'm going to ask you to remember them for me. All right?"

I nodded anxiously. My first test of mental functioning. What deficit might it reveal?

"Here they are," she said. "Rose. Lilac. Geranium. Orchid." She slowly counted them off on her fingers. "Do you have that?"

I nodded again, frowning as I repeated them mentally and struggled mightily to retain them in my mind. Remembering such things used to be so easy for me—I had all the telephone numbers in my address book committed to memory—but my mind was now such a fog, remembering was like trying to swim through molasses.

The physical exam continued. She tested the strength—or rather weakness—of my legs, my ankles, and my neck, and had me close my eyes while she bent my thumbs to see if I could distinguish up from down. I could. This faculty, she explained, was vital. Without the ability to sense where my body parts were without looking, rehabilitation would have been much more difficult.

Another ten minutes had now elapsed. I had forgotten all about the flowers when Dr. Doherty paused and said, "Ready to remember the flowers?"

The flowers! What were they? Rose, that was one. What were the others?

Since I couldn't talk, she read several off a list, asking me to signal which ones were one of the original four.

"Dahlia."

I shook my head.

"Lilac."

Was that one? I thought so and nodded.

The test continued. To my surprise, I was able to recall three out of four.

"Great," she said finally, scribbling on her clipboard. "You'll do fine." A little more scribbling, and then she announced, "I think you'll be able to recover a hundred percent."

A hundred percent? Her words were a shock. Amy had told me at Marin General that the doctors there were optimistic, but this was different. This was a pronouncement coming from an expert. How could she know? I groped for my alphabet board.

"R-E-A-L-L-Y?" I spelled out. Dr. Doherty leaned down, following my pointing finger.

She laughed, a lovely, musical sound. "Really!"

"How ... do ... you ... know?" I spelled.

"I've seen a lot of viral encephalitis. You may think you're in bad shape, but believe me, I've seen much worse. If you work hard, you'll make a good recovery."

I lifted my left hand and made a fist. Yes, of course. I would work hard.

And then I spelled out the sixty-four-dollar question: "W-H-E-N?"

She laughed again and patted me on the shoulder. "Rome wasn't built in a day. It will take time. But if all goes well, by December most of your healing should be done."

None of us knew it then, but my healing would not progress nearly as smoothly as she had implied. The future held much surprise and difficulty, but for now, I was thrilled.

She continued, "We have four main goals for you here. First is to get rid of your 'trach' so you can eat and talk."

Trach (pronounced "trake") was hospital shorthand for tracheostomy, the breathing hole and plastic device in my throat through which I breathed.

"Second, we have make sure your swallowing works so we can take out your G-tube [the feeding tube that had been inserted directly into my stomach] and you can eat. Third, you need to regain control of your bodily functions. And fourth, you have to learn how to walk again."

I could barely raise my head or move my arms. Was it really possible?

Dr. Doherty saw the doubt etched in my face.

"That's right," she repeated emphatically. "The day you leave here, you'll walk out."

At the moment it seemed inconceivable.

"Your physical therapists will start you on your program tomorrow morning. Remember, the harder you work, the faster you'll heal. All right?"

I gave her a thumbs-up sign. Bring them on. I was ready.

"I'll see you tomorrow."

Then with a jaunty wave she was gone, and Greta was already wrapping a tourniquet on my arm, in preparation for taking blood. "You'll valk," she said. "Dr. Doherty knows. She can always tell. Dr. Doherty is a great doctor. You'll see."

I wanted to believe it. Dr. Doherty's prognosis had transformed my attitude from confusion to one of genuine excitement. I was elated, floating on air. One hundred percent! I would move heaven and earth to make that happen.

Amy could sense my newfound enthusiasm and gently stroked my hair. "You see, it's going to be all right. Really, it is."

Suddenly, it was all too much. I burst into tears.

The next day two women entered my curtained space and introduced themselves as Annette and Jean, my physical therapists for the day. They sat on the bed, one on either side of me. With my double vision, each of them appeared to be two people.

"We're going to check how well your tongue works, and then see if we can get you sitting up. Okay?" said Annette.

I nodded.

Annette brought a small object close to my face. "Open your mouth." I did, and felt a strange sensation in the middle of my face, as though my skin were being pulled apart. She inserted a lemon-flavored swab into my mouth and asked me to move my tongue around it. The sensation of flavor hit me with the force of a bomb. So this was my mouth. It felt all wrong, like a foreign, gaping hole in my face. For the first time, I understood that while I had been able to think and spell words for the last few days, my tactile sense and body image were grossly distorted.

Next they slid their hands under my back and shoulders and started to lift. I came up a few inches. They adjusted, instructing each other as they went. "You take the shoulder." "Watch his arm, watch his arm." I felt the pressure of my body's dead weight against their grip and began to slip back. "Watch out, he's leaning left!"

Finally they had their grip right and brought me up. I felt the room start to spin. Aside from one abortive effort by a physical therapist back at Marin General, this was the first time my body had been upright in weeks, and I felt as though I had been transported through a vast, dizzying space.

"We've got you," Jean said, their arms all around me, gripping me hard. My legs must have been askew, but it was only when Annette reached down to untangle them that I knew it. I couldn't sense their position relative to each other.

"Are you all right?" Annette asked.

I mouthed the word "Yes" but couldn't feel my mouth doing it.

What was this huge weight, like a bowling ball, pressing against my chest? I tried to reach up with my hand to find out what it was, but the two of them were holding me by the shoulders, and I couldn't. It was only when Jean reached out herself and touched the "bowling ball" that I realized with dismay that it was my head. I hadn't known what it was. As with my legs, I could feel Jean touch my head but not its place on my body. It was pressing against

my chest because my neck muscles were too weak to hold
it up.

They held me there only for a few moments, but I was
already starting to slip from their grasp. "Do you want to
lie down again?" I mouthed "Yes" frantically.

Very slowly, adjusting their grip each inch of the way,
working in tandem like two piano movers, they eased me
down until I was back in bed, safe at last, lying on my
back—the only posture I had known for weeks, and the
only one, I now realized, I was capable of. Lying immobile, pointing to letters on an alphabet board, living only
through my mind, I had had the sense that I was not so
bad off. Now that illusion, as well as the excitement I
had felt the previous day with Dr. Doherty, had been
destroyed in those few moments with Annette and Jean.
Now I knew the truth. I was a basket case. I needed two
people to help me sit up. I didn't know I had a mouth. I
thought my head was a bowling ball. I hadn't the strength
even to lift it off my chest.

I lay there, stunned, trying to absorb the enormity of
it all.

Unbeknownst to me, Amy had been watching Jean and
Annette working with me from the door of my room. She
saw my terrible weakness, the way my head hung uselessly
against my chest. It was too much for her too. She went
out to the car and cried.

And alone in my curtained cubicle, I also cried. The
truth of my condition had finally hit home, and I was
overcome.

When they had first met, Amy had asked Dr. Doherty if I could have a private room. Now, once Amy and the doctor understood how much my first therapy had affected me, Dr. Doherty agreed that my emotional as well as physical needs would be better served if I had my own space. Within a couple of days it was done, and once again, as at Marin General, the view from my bed featured a wall clock (or rather two clocks, due to my double vision) and the door to the bathroom, though I would not be using it for some time. To the left of the bed was a sliding glass door through which, when the curtains were opened during the day, I could see a tile-paved courtyard. And above the courtyard roof were the swaying top branches of a row of eucalyptus trees. To the right of my bed was a built-in bureau of drawers and a closet. Farther to the right lay another, empty bed, along with some hospital equipment, but I could barely turn my head far enough to see it. Until I could be lifted into a wheelchair, this was to be my entire world. Like Alice yearning to enter the forbidden garden of Wonderland, I ached to be able to cross those few feet from my bed to those drawers and see what was in them. They were so close, yet so far.

From that day on I burst into tears over every little thing, or nothing at all. This was not like me. Or not as I used to be. I was ashamed by this weepiness, and also confused. Why was I so sad and emotional? I should be happy. I had just received the best possible news from my doctor, news that could have been so much worse. I knew people who had had strokes. I saw the effect that had on their emotions, and how easily and often they cried. So when Dr. Doherty explained to me that any brain trauma caused its victim to become emotionally labile for a time, it came as no surprise. Some of what I was experiencing could be attributed to that, I thought, but not all. What about this profound sense of loss that gnawed at my belly? Since at this point I could not express my feelings verbally, all Amy could do was hold me while the tears flowed, and remind me over and over that I was going to get better. Hadn't Dr. Doherty said so? Amy was tireless in her efforts to comfort me, but she herself did not share my sadness. On the contrary, what she felt was relief and happiness—happiness that I had survived, joy that I would recover, elation that the worst of the nightmare would soon be over. This difference between her mood and mine would remain a puzzle to her until the day I regained my speech, and could finally explain to her what I was feeling inside. Only then would she understand that, at the moment, emotionally we were living in two different realities.

Nighttime was the hardest, when Amy had to leave, my one link to my former life. At first all I could do was hug her, and convey through gestures and scrawled notes how much I loved her. That was until I invented the bedtime routine I called "Be Lenny."

The idea came to me when I was lying in bed one afternoon, alone, contemplating my future, and the phrase popped into my head, "Tell me how it's gonna be, Lenny." This is of course the oft-repeated plea of George, the retarded giant, in John Steinbeck's *Of Mice and Men*. His friend Lenny had dreams of buying a farm someday for George and himself, and George never tired of hearing from Lenny about these plans, about "how it's gonna be."

And so, every evening, just as Amy was ready to leave, I would write on my notepad, or later, say to her, "Be Lenny." And because we had played this game for many nights now already, she knew exactly what to do and say.

She took her place at my bedside, held my hands, looked directly into my eyes, and began to speak in the tone of a mother telling her child a bedtime story. Each day the story would be the same. "You had a good day today. You're getting better and better. Soon you'll be able to sit in a wheelchair. Then you'll be able to use a walker, and we'll be able to go for walks together. Next you'll be able to use a cane. As soon as you can walk well enough, they'll send you home. You'll sleep in your own bed, and I'll cook meals for you, and we'll take walks every day, and you'll continue to go to physical therapy, and your friends will come to visit, and before you know it you'll be all better."

In the silence that would follow, she could see that I wanted her to tell me more. And she would oblige, stringing out these little vignettes of my future for as long as she could.

I needed these stories. I wanted to picture myself as I once was, not in this place of sickness, but in my own home where I was once again myself, a functioning human being. And so I urged her to go on, as long as I could think of things to ask and she of things to say.

This little ritual gave me great comfort. For those few moments, I suppose I was indeed the child, and she the mother, and all the fears and the anxieties of the day would melt away. When she finished, I would feel a pang of regret, because I knew after the long day, after all our time together, at last it was time for her to go.

After a final kiss and hug, she was gone, and I lay awake in the dark trying to sleep, though it was hard, even with pills. Even when sleep finally came, it did not feel normal or restful, but more like a jagged swoon, as though my brain were being rubbed with sandpaper. And of course I could only sleep in one position—on my back—since I lacked the strength to turn on my side. It was a sign of my lingering mental confusion that for many days I attributed this problem to some curious limitation of the bed, rather than my own weakness.

I would often lie awake far into the night, remembering all the things Amy said, repeating to myself over and over, like a prayer, "I will get better. I will get better." Later, when I could lift my hands far enough, I would press them into my temples and try to visualize my brain surrounded by the traditional Buddhist blue light of healing. "I will get better."

My sadness was not all about inner loss. My external physical symptoms, though not life-threatening, were disturbing, especially my double vision and the stripes of numbness all over my body that made me feel like a neurological zebra. The lack of sensation in my face was particularly disconcerting. Sometimes I would touch it to assure myself that it was still there. And on awakening, I could not tell where my arms and legs were until I moved them. Dr. Doherty explained that what gives us our sense of physical existence is really nothing more than the brain stem interpreting a mass of nerve signals continuously being sent from all over the body. All she would say when I asked her when it would improve was, "It will go away in time." But when? She couldn't say.

But of all my symptoms, the one that bothered me the most was the distortion of vision and hearing that I called the "fog." When we awaken from a dream, we know immediately that we are in the "real" world. Our eyes, ears, our body, our whole nervous system, tell us that we are awake and that what is around us is real. In the fog I lacked that quality. Intellectually I knew I was awake, but my senses kept telling me I was dreaming. Visual objects were too bright, too vivid, and seemed to glow with danger. Even from a few feet away, Amy or Dr. Doherty appeared faint and distant. Low-frequency sounds were ominously loud, so much so that I often had trouble hearing people's voices. The sound of a vacuum cleaner, or of the air-conditioning, felt like the growling of a dangerous animal.

Every day I concocted some excuse to ask Dr. Doherty about this fog, probing her medical knowledge, struggling to understand. "It will clear," she said emphatically. It was only when I pressed her that she explained further. "You're unusually perceptive," she said. "Most patients aren't able to sense these things clearly, or articulate them the way you do. They don't recognize their mental confusion until it lifts, and then they are amazed. You seem to be able to sense it while it's happening."

Even so, I wasn't sure my fog was like these other patients' experiences, or that Dr. Doherty really understood exactly what I was experiencing. I felt isolated and alone in my fun-house-mirror prison.

Thankfully, I was in no physical pain. All the suffering I felt was in my mind. And as I was to find out soon enough, I was in better shape than most of the other patients in the neurological ward. My Buddhist training had taught me that our deepest suffering is mental and is ultimately caused by our attachment to the self, to being, to existence. The purpose of Buddhist meditation is to experience the self in silence, hour after hour, month after month, until it reveals itself not as a solid, permanent entity, like a stone statue, but a mere flickering mental construct. In this way we reduce our clinging to it, and thus our suffering. I had thought that through my years of meditation I had learned this lesson well, but after this near-death experience and loss of identity I had to admit to myself how deeply attached I still was to the old "me," and how much I wanted it back. This illness was a spiritual lesson of a different order entirely—not a meditation exercise, but the real deal. It only made me more miserable to realize that my Buddhist understanding was not as deep or thorough as I had thought. One more piece of my identity shredded—or so it seemed.

I should have remembered the story I told in chapter 2 about the time Shunryu Suzuki nearly drowned in the swimming hole near the Tassajara monastery. Even a Buddhist master as developed as he was not immune from some fear of death, some lingering attachment to survive, to be, to continue, as he explained to us without an ounce of shame. To him the only shame was any notion of being permanently an expert, a master. "Beginner's Mind" was his favorite teaching, the title of his one published book, and, he said, the secret to understanding Buddhism. Even a master such as he, he taught, was a beginner in the face of each new moment. But lying in my hospital bed, drowning not in water but in my own grief, I had forgotten such profound spiritual lessons. I only remembered that I once was so strong, physically and mentally, and now, I thought, oh so weak.

As I lay in bed, watching the minutes tick by on my doubled wall clock, it did occur to me to try some basic Buddhist meditation practices. I tried mindfulness, which is to simply note, dispassionately, whatever is happening in the mind: "Now I am grieving. Now I am feeling grief." I also tried to yoke that thought to my breathing, since the breath is the basis of achieving a calm, stable state of mind. Once these practices would have calmed and centered me. But now the voice of my mindful thinking seemed weak as a whisper in a hurricane. And my breathing, like so much else in my body, didn't seem to be connected to anything I could call "me." I could feel my belly rise and fall, but it felt external to myself, like the clock or the curtains. After so many years of familiarity and long practice, I could not find any calm in these spiritual exercises. In fact their failure only intensified my distress.

Only with Amy could I find any solace. Two weeks into my stay, my trach was removed, a momentous event I will recount in more detail in chapter 6. From then on I could finally talk, but all I could seem to talk about was my grief and despair, and my fear that my mind was damaged, or that I would fail to recover as Dr. Doherty had predicted. I was like someone standing on the ledge of a thirty-story building. No matter how many times I was told I would not fall, and that over time the building would shrink in height until I could stand on terra firma like anyone else, the sensation of danger was too strong.

From this time forward Amy had to absorb these complaints from me constantly, and although she did it with patience and good spirits, as time passed I became worried at the toll it must be taking on her. Eventually I felt, for her sake as well as mine, that I needed an outside professional to help me deal with my emotional storm.

So through friends I contacted a warmhearted psychiatrist, who in turn referred me to his colleague, a lovely woman named Diane, who had been a registered nurse before becoming a psychotherapist specializing in helping people with serious illness. From our first meeting, I was drawn to her natural empathy. With blond curls and a delicate, gentle face, she was someone I felt I could confide in. I had never engaged in psychotherapy before; once I would have rejected it as something unnecessary. Now I craved it, as she began to lead me through the grieving process.

Our first session consisted mostly of my tears.

"I'm sorry," I sobbed, "I just can't stop crying. I don't know why. I should be happy that I survived. Why can't I feel that?"

"You don't need to apologize," she replied in a gentle voice. "You've been through an awful experience. You nearly died. Don't be ashamed of those tears or try to hold them back. Each one of those tears is golden. Each one is cleansing you, helping you to heal."

Still, I was ashamed of my crying. I considered it weak and childish. I had never cried much, even as a child, and certainly not as an adult. This flood of emotion felt to me like a loss of control, a breakdown, and I told her so.

"No," she corrected me. "No. It's not a breakdown. It's just feeling, deep feeling. Let it come."

In a later session, Diane asked me to tell her the whole history of my illness, especially when I was just emerging from my coma.

"I couldn't move," I said, my voice quavering from the memory. "I couldn't talk. The nurses would come and put a suction tube in the hole in my throat. Each time it made me choke so much I thought I was going to die. I didn't understand why they were torturing me. Amy said she explained it all to me, again and again, but I didn't understand."

"That must have been terrible!" Diane replied. After a pause to consider, she added, "Perhaps what you are feeling now are the emotions you felt then, but couldn't express. Sometimes the feelings we have during a traumatic experience take time to catch up with us."

Yes, that made sense—that terrible fear, that incomprehension and disorientation. Perhaps only now had I begun to experience it emotionally. I no longer felt quite so ashamed, quite so weak. Perhaps my tears were normal after all.

As we became better acquainted and Diane began to probe more deeply into my grieving, she began to draw me out about my life before the illness.

"When grief appears, it doesn't exist in a vacuum. There's a connection with other times of grief in your life, other sadness."

Other times of grief. I thought back. "My mother died when I was four." There it was, that simple declarative sentence, but I knew it was the primal tragedy of my life.

"Four!" Diane exclaimed. "That's a terrible time for a boy to lose his mother. What do you remember about that?"

"Not much," I answered truthfully. It was buried deep in the recesses of my unconscious. But was it surfacing now? I felt a chill go down my spine. If so, I was not sure I was ready to face that on top of everything else.

Diane sensed my discomfort. "What other times have you grieved?"

I told her about the death of my beloved Buddhist teacher, how I cried and cried at his funeral. I told of my bout with cancer, and a time years later when I had an emergency operation for an obstructed gallbladder, and feared my cancer had returned. I mentioned the recent deaths of both my parents.

"But I didn't grieve about my cancer," I added. "I was upbeat most of the time."

She listened intently as I concluded my recital of personal setbacks. "Sometimes," she replied, after a short silence, "we can only tolerate so much adversity in our life, and then something happens that brings it all to a head, the straw that breaks the camel's back. This illness may be like that for you."

Perhaps she was right. More than a straw, though. More like a ton of bricks.

Even with Diane's twice-weekly visits, I was still concerned that Amy was having to absorb too much of my emotional outpourings, and worried that I was becoming too much of a burden to her.

"Is Amy all right?" I asked Diane after each session. "She has to put up with so much from me. Would you talk with her before you leave? Check to make sure she is all right?"

Diane did that, and continued to assure me that Amy was holding up fine. "I don't think you have to worry," she told me. "She's a very strong person, and she loves you very much."

"I know," I said. "I know."

It seemed to me that my grief could not possibly end, that it would go on forever. I should have remembered that everything changes, nothing persists indefinitely, but it is the hallmark of depressive states like sadness and grief that they seem to be set in stone for all time.

But already, without my realizing it, my grief was beginning to mutate and transform itself. There is a well-known Buddhist story that illustrates this point most beautifully, the story of the mustard seed. A woman comes to the Buddha holding her newly deceased baby, overcome with grief, and says, "Lord Buddha, I have heard that you are the wisest of men. You see that my only child, my beloved child, has died in my arms. Please bring him back to life for me."

The Buddha responded, "First I need you to do something for me. I would like you to visit each household of the neighboring villages and towns, and collect one mustard seed from each dwelling place that has been free from a tragedy similar to yours. Bring those mustard seeds back to me, and then we will see." And so the woman did as the Buddha said.

I was like that woman, carrying my grief from day to day just as she carried her dead baby in her arms from town to town, household to household. What the woman discovered in her search, and what the Buddha taught her when she returned, is the subject of the next chapter, where I will recount the conclusion of the mustard seed story and my own awakening to the place that grief can eventually carry us—toward gratitude and compassion.

FIVE

GRATITUDE AND COMPASSION

Lazarus lies in bed, helpless to move. But he sees now that he is not alone. His wife is with him, as well as his relatives and friends. They stroke his limbs and speak soothing words into his ear. Lazarus finds his heart filled with such gratitude for their care, and for even simpler things—the light streaming in from the window, the warmth of the fire in the hearth, the sight of his own two hands held before his face. How wonderful it was to be alive! How wonderful to be surrounded by loved ones who are always there for you, whatever happens.

My period of grieving at Kentfield continued. Intellectually, I knew I should be thankful that I had survived. But I was like a ship with all topsail and no keel. Beneath that thin layer of intact cognition lay the broken hull of my ravaged nervous system and my nearly useless body. Before I could find the thread to lead me away from grief and toward gratitude, I had to relearn a lesson from my study of Buddhism: suffering is not a cruel trick of fate, it is simply an unavoidable fact of human life.

In the last chapter I told the first half of the Buddhist story of the woman with the dead child and the mustard seed. The grieving woman, wandering from house to house with her dead child in her arms, represented how I felt trapped in my sorrow, searching desperately for some relief. Now I will tell the conclusion of this tale, which illustrates how grief finds solace in gratitude, compassion, and love.

The woman, trusting in the Buddha's wisdom, wandered from village to village, her face covered with tears, to find that one mustard seed from a house free from a tragedy similar to her own. When she finally returned, after many days of wandering, the Buddha could immediately see from the expression on her face that something had changed.

"Did you bring the mustard seeds as I asked you?" the Buddha inquired.

"Lord Buddha," the woman answered, "I went to every household in the area, but I could not find a single one where some tragedy like mine had not at some time befallen them. I have no mustard seeds for you, but I have learned something that I did not know before. Whatever darkness or ill fortune has befallen my life, I should be grateful for what I still have. That is what the villagers in their houses all told me. Though my baby has died, I can still have other children, and I am filled with gratitude at that possibility. You are indeed wise, even wiser than they say."

And with that the woman departed, having learned a lesson that we each have to face in life. And now it was my turn.

I still could not control my frequent weeping. And at first I interpreted all of my crying in the same way—as tears of sadness and mourning. It was only gradually that I realized my weeping had different causes. When two nurses would come into my room to pull my body back up on the bed after I had slid down so far that my feet were hanging over it, I would mouth the words "Thank you" to them each time with tears in my eyes, tears not of grief but of appreciation for their simple acts of kindness.

Another opportunity for me to recognize the gratitude germinating within me was my relationship with Amy. We had been high school and college sweethearts, and had married in our senior year of college. She had been with me through my year in seminary and all my years of study and teaching at the San Francisco Zen Center. We were together during my first career as a business executive, including the shock of losing my job there as that business was sold, and the trials and tribulations of starting my own business. Thirty-two years of happy marriage.

Yet she had always been her own person. With a master's degree in early childhood education, she had pursued her own career in teaching, from kindergarten teacher to school principal, before retiring in 1998 to enjoy a well-deserved rest, a period that had unexpectedly culminated in this terrible situation.

Had she still been employed, my time in the hospital would have been much more lonely and difficult. As it happened, from the beginning she was able to be with me for much of each day. She also handled all the negotiations with doctors, insurance companies, and the hospital administration, as well as keeping our wide circle of friends informed through telephone and e-mail. Though we had always been committed to mutual respect and independence in our marriage, during the last year my various enterprises had dominated our day-to-day existence. Now suddenly our roles were reversed. She was in charge of every aspect of our lives, and managed it all brilliantly under crushing stress.

Each day when she walked through the door of my hospital room and set down her backpack with a cheery greeting, the sight of her face was sheer joy. My love for her and gratitude for her presence were now being intensified by hitherto untapped forces from deep in my heart. We had spent our whole adult life together and yet, as deep as our love had grown, this crisis had taken it still deeper. When I was with her, my body, otherwise so numb and devoid of much sensation, was flooded with strong physical sensations of gratitude.

One day, shortly after I had regained my speech, I asked her to tell me once again all that had happened in intensive care while I was unconscious, a story I needed to hear and never tired of hearing. She described how, even after it was clear I would survive, the doctors cautioned her that I might awaken paralyzed or permanently brain damaged—"A body with no brain, or a brain with no body," is how one of them put it. Such a chilling thought.

"How did you feel when they told you that?" I asked.

"I was prepared for it," she said.

"You mean no matter what happened, whatever condition I was in?"

"Of course," she said, surprised that I would even think to ask. "You're my husband. You're my Lew. I love you."

After thirty-two years, only now did I fully appreciate the depth of that love. All I could do was beckon her to me, and reach up from the bed as best I could with my so-weak arms to embrace her for a long time.

One of the first things Amy had done when I moved to my private room was hang a painting of the Medicine Buddha on the wall at the foot of my bed, where I could always see it. One of our treasured household possessions, it portrayed the Buddha as a healer, his body colored the traditional deep blue of lapis lazuli, holding a jar of medicine in his hand with a healing flower emerging from it.

Since then, I had occasionally used the painting to practice the Medicine Buddha meditation, first visualizing a healing energy in the heart of the Medicine Buddha himself and then imagining that energy flowing into my own heart, circling counterclockwise in time with the breath. But with gratitude now beginning to grow in my heart, I returned to the practice in earnest, and no longer just as an exercise. Now it was authenticated by something tangible, the full power of our married love. Though I had done this practice many times on behalf of others, now I finally understood the energy that drove it, and made it effective and real. It was gratitude.

About a week after my first physical therapy session, the one in which my head hung against my chest like a bowling ball, I was able to sit in a wheelchair for short periods, although I still needed two strong nurses to get me into it. In a few days my sitting time had increased to half an hour, at which point I was eager to have Amy take me on a tour of the hospital, at last to emerge from the cocoon of my room and see a little of the world outside it.

The hospital was not large, just a double quadrangle of hallways that were a bustle of activity—nurses entering and leaving patient rooms, visitors coming and going, patients on crutches and canes. By now I had come to understand that there were three units in the hospital.

Units 1 and 2 were for patients whose injuries were mostly physical—broken bones, broken hips, broken backs, and so on. Unit 3, my unit, was the neurological ward, where the stroke and brain trauma victims were housed.

After one circuit of the hallways, I was dizzy with overload from my sensory fog, and motioned to Amy to return me to my room. But even in this short tour I could see for myself the condition of the other patients in my unit. Many of them lay in bed, immobile, some surrounded by complex machinery. Amy said these were the long-term coma victims, ones who were unlikely to awaken—ever. I had my first look at the gymnasium, two rooms filled with raised mats, parallel bars, and other equipment, where people lay on mats next to their therapists, struggling to perform the simplest of motions. And we passed a few patients like me, touring the hallway in their wheelchairs or walkers.

On this first trip around the quadrangle I was like the woman in the Buddhist story of the mustard seed, carrying my grief as she carried her dead child. But the suffering I saw as Amy wheeled me along touched me deeply. With Dr. Doherty's magic words—"You will recover one hundred percent"—echoing in my ears, I felt humbled. As awful as I felt, as debilitated as I was, I was clearly more fortunate than many of the people I saw.

My sorrow over my lost identity by no means disappeared, but it changed its color that day. Grief's stronger companion—gratitude—had now been awakened in my heart. Now I felt, as well as grief, thanks to be alive. I had lost a lot, but not all. The part of me that really mattered was still alive, and my tour through the tiny "village" of the hospital, like the journey the woman made in the Buddhist story, had served to remind me of that precious fact. The unfortunate souls I saw as I traveled, the ones trapped in bodies and minds that would never fully heal, were my teachers that day.

Later, particularly after I could talk, I discovered that the nurses in Unit 3 could be my teachers too. Their difficult work with neurological patients was more than a job for them. It was a calling. One of them was Maria, a Mexican American with a face of rugged beauty and stoic strength. One day, as she was changing my bedsheets, we began conversing, and her story came out.

"You'll get better," she told me, "if you have faith. When I was a girl, in Mexico, I was in bed for three years. Three whole years. I was in so much pain, I prayed every night for God not to let me die, but please just to take away some of the pain."

"Three years!" I repeated. I was stunned. I had been in my bed for all of three weeks. "What did you have?"

"Rheumatic fever."

"Couldn't they give you drugs for the pain?"

"There were no drugs. My parents said to pray to God, and never lose faith that someday I would get better."

"Three years." I was still trying to imagine it. "How old were you?"

"Sixteen, seventeen." She paused, then added, "Sometimes the hardest things in life make us stronger." She snapped the sheet over my body and began tucking it in. "Have patience. Have faith. I know."

Now I understood why Maria had such an aura of inner strength, and why she had chosen to do this difficult work. I also felt chastened by her tale. Yes, I had survived a brush with death, but I was in no pain, nothing like this woman had had to endure when only a child. I vowed to keep her story in mind.

Josephine, a nurse with a cheery grin and an infectious optimism, confided in me one day that she had chosen to work here at Kentfield because of how well they had taken care of her father when he had a stroke. "This is one of the best facilities in the country, you know," she said. "When my father had his stroke, I checked around."

"And that's why you're here?"

"That, and of course, Dr. Doherty."

Like many of the staff, Josephine seemed to look on Dr. Doherty as a kind of miracle worker, and indeed I could see, just from the way the doctor went about her work, that her dedication to her patients was absolute. Once while I was sitting in my wheelchair, near the nurses' station, I watched her sit down next to an elderly stroke victim, seemingly oblivious to the crowd of nurses buzzing around her, all trying to get her attention.

"I'm Dr. Doherty," she said to the patient, enunciating each syllable slowly. "Now. Who am I?"

The patient didn't respond.

"I'm Dr. Doherty," she said again. "Who am I?"

She repeated this over and over, for some minutes, until the patient finally mumbled, "Dr. Doherty."

"Good!" Dr. Doherty said, beaming. "That's right. I'm Dr. Doherty."

It was only then that she rose, turned around, and began responding to all the questions the nurses around her were waiting to ask.

After a couple of weeks of Amy rolling me on daily tours through the hospital halls, during which I regained my speech and began to practice eating, she asked if I wanted to go outside. Immediately I felt a pang of apprehension. When I had first arrived, my zone of safety was no larger than my bed. That zone had been slowly expanding to include my wheelchair and room, and now, the interior hallways. But outside? That felt like too risky a leap. After some consideration, though, I decided to try it. I realized I now wanted to see more of the world than the view from my room or the familiar hospital corridors. I wanted the reassurance that the wide world was still there, waiting for me, and that it was a place to which I could someday return.

So down the hallway Amy pushed me as I leaned forward and clutched the armrests of my wheelchair. The front doors to the hospital slid open automatically as we bumped over the threshold and out into the sunlight of the hospital parking lot. The light was blinding, and the low-frequency sounds of a nearby air conditioning vent sounded like a jet plane to me. When Amy leaned down and asked me if I was okay, I found it hard to hear her voice over this ominous rumbling in my ears.

I nodded dubiously.

"Are you sure?" she repeated, seeing my face tight with tension.

I nodded again, then cocked my head. "What's that?" I said as we moved into the parking lot. "There's another roaring sound, over there. " I pointed to some trees.

She didn't know what I meant. "Maybe the traffic," she ventured. "The highway is just on the other side of those trees."

The wheelchair rattled on the rough asphalt of the parking lot as she turned me onto a path that led through a parklike area, with trees and shrubs on one side and a fenced, trickling creek on the other. My first outside landscape, lit up like a firecracker by my hypersensitive vision, was wonderful nonetheless. I twisted and turned in the wheelchair as we rolled along, trying to take it all in.

Along the way we passed a blackberry bush. I love blackberries, and near our home in Mill Valley there was a whole hillside of them, lining the road where Amy and I would take our daily walks. I always looked forward each year to the late summertime, when we could pause in our walk by the blackberry bushes, stand by the roadside, and feast on them. Now it was again that season.

"Are there any ripe ones left?" I asked.

She reached high up, picked a few, and brought them down to me. I took only one and put it in my mouth. Such sweetness! And sorrow too, remembering those previous summers when I was healthy and could pick blackberries by myself.

Then came an even darker feeling, an echo of the grief still alive in my heart as I realized here, outside the protection and safety of the hospital, how disabled I was, and how long a road I would need to travel before I could begin to function again in this world of such fresh, sparkling beauty.

Grief and gratitude, twin emotions engendering the same physical reaction: tears.

"Let's go back," I said, wiping my wet cheeks with the back of my hand.

"What's wrong?" Amy said.

"It's wonderful," I replied, "but it's enough for now." I reached up and gripped her hand. "It's enough."

On our way back through the parking lot, I held a hand over one eye and looked for our car, the white Honda Accord that had been mine until I became ill, and which Amy was now using instead of her older Civic. But the row upon row of cars were a blur. I couldn't find ours.

"Where's the car?" I asked, and she pointed, then rolled me over to it.

I touched it, felt its cold metal, and peered against my cupped hands through the window. I saw it all—the steering wheel, the gearshift, the power window controls, once such a familiar part of my daily life, and now so far beyond my capability. I'm sure I didn't even have the strength to open the door.

"Okay," I said, and motioned for her to turn me away. I

had seen enough. The car was an old friend, but one I would not be able to meet for a long time yet. "Let's go back inside."

A story in Buddhist scripture illustrates the preciousness of human life. There is a solitary turtle, the story goes, with one eye in the middle of its belly, whose greatest wish in life is to see the most wonderful thing in the world—the sun. But how can he do it when he must always swim facedown in the ocean deeps? Well, suppose, the story continues, there is one wooden board with a hole in its center in the entire ocean, just the right size for a turtle to turn belly up and grasp with its four legs, to see the sun at last with his single eye. What are the chances that the solitary turtle will ever meet up with such a board? So, the story concludes, is the chance of our being born into this human life. We should, therefore, be as grateful as that turtle that we have this life.

As we left the hospital for this first excursion, out through the sliding doors of the hospital into the blinding sunlight, I felt just like that turtle. For the first time since my return to life, I had reached up, held on, and seen the sun. I couldn't hold on for very long, but for the first time I understood this teaching tale, which I had told for so years in my lectures, from the vantage point of the turtle.

That evening I concocted a little rhyme: "I'm grateful for my life, I'm grateful for my wife." It was the first of many such phrases that I would use in the coming weeks and months to evoke and remember the feeling of this day.

• • •

At the beginning of my stay at Kentfield, I did not want to have any visitors, even though all my friends kept asking Amy when they could see me. Just coping with my own situation was difficult enough, without trying to handle company. But when Amy told me that Jack, the Buddhist teacher who had visited me in the intensive care ward, wanted to see me again, I readily agreed. I realized I wanted and needed to see him.

And so in due time he came. I prepared for the visit by dressing in the best clothes I had and was sitting up in my wheelchair, a blanket over my knees, when he arrived. As soon as he came through the door he came right over, leaned down, and gave me a big hug.

"Well," were his first words, "you're certainly looking better than the last time I saw you!"

Yes, back then I couldn't speak or move. I couldn't even put my hands together in the traditional Buddhist greeting. This time I could, and did.

Then we sat together, Amy, Jack, and I, in silence. Jack closed his eyes and entered meditation. Finally he opened his eyes, sighed deeply, and said, "You don't feel to me as though you are completely in your body yet." He looked at me questioningly. "How does it feel to you?"

Yes, that was exactly what I had been trying in my incoherent way to express to Amy and Dr. Doherty for some time. I was still slowly reinhabiting my body from a time during my coma when I was not in it at all. It was not just the lack of physical sensation or the bizarre disturbance of my vision and hearing—the symptoms I had been talking about—but something more fundamental. That must be why I looked and sounded to others so much better than I felt inside, and I was grateful to Jack, with his insight both as a meditation master and as a psychologist, for so accurately describing my condition.

"What do you think I should do?" I asked. Perhaps Jack knew some meditative technique that would hasten my reembodiment.

He just smiled gently. "I think it will just take time, Lew," he said. "Give it time."

As after his previous visit, I felt so grateful for Jack's kind presence and care.

My next visitor was Roger, also a Buddhist teacher as well as a professor of psychiatry. In my coma dreams he was the one making comments at the shamanistic bird ceremony, though in the flesh he was a most warm, considerate person and a dear friend. All the time I was in intensive care he telephoned Amy every day to check on my condition.

Since the day was bright and sunny, we all adjourned to the hospital's outside wooden deck for our visit. Roger began by delivering some good news. Although organic brain disease was not his specialty, he had researched my condition in his medical texts, and from one he quoted the following phrase to me: "Regarding viral encephalitis in the brain stem, recovery is long but usually complete." That cheered me up a good bit, since I had been pestering Dr. Doherty every day to reassure me that I really truly was going to recover fully, as she said.

"You think I've changed my mind since yesterday?" she would joke with me.

But now Roger, my trusted friend, had confirmed her prognosis. Hearing this bit of encouragement, I was momentarily elated, but soon I shifted the conversation to the topic that was so much on my mind—my sensory fog—hoping that Roger, with his medical as well as meditative knowledge, might have some fresh insight.

"Everything is too bright," I explained. "Sounds are too loud. It doesn't feel real. It's like a waking nightmare. Or being on a psychedelic drug trip that never ends. What do you think it is? What's wrong with me?"

"Some aftereffect of the disease, undoubtedly," Roger replied. "Remember, it nearly killed you, and there's a lot of neurological repair work to be done. It sounds to me as though you've lost your filtering."

I asked him to explain.

"From the time we're infants, our brain slowly learns to filter sensory perception in a way that makes the world comprehensible, so instead of just seeing colored shapes and hearing random sounds, we can organize the world into recognizable objects. Psychedelic drugs are one way to temporarily lift that filter, which is why Aldous Huxley called them 'the doors of perception.' It may be the encephalitis has done somewhat the same thing."

"How long will it last, do you think?" Several weeks had now gone by, and I had not seen any signs that the fog was abating.

"I don't think there's any set time frame for this kind of

healing. However long it takes for your brain stem to heal itself. And it will, I'm sure. All in due time."

I sighed. That was what Dr. Doherty had said too. There were to be no magic answers, even from Roger. My healing would take as long as it would take. And there was nothing, it seemed, that I or anyone else could do about it.

That night I recalled what my Buddhist teacher Shunryu Suzuki said when he was dying of cancer: "Cancer is my friend." That statement so deeply impressed me then that now, nearly thirty years later, it inspired me to make up a new phrase to repeat to myself: "The fog is my friend, and it's going away. The fog is my friend, and it's going away." That wasn't literally true, not yet anyway, but if cancer could be Suzuki's friend, then the fog could be mine. As his ordained disciple, this effort, I thought, was the least I could do.

Soon I felt ready for more visitors, especially my two business partners, Mary and Jalal. They had visited me before, when I was in intensive care, but then I was so weak I could hardly recognize them. Since coming to Kentfield, we had spoken from time to time on the telephone, but now at last I could thank them in person for their extraordinary efforts to keep the business running smoothly in my absence. I was delighted to see them, and they me. The past few weeks had been a difficult time for all three of us, and this get-together was a kind of celebration.

Propped up on pillows in bed, I spread my arms and said, "Well, Jalal, you were right. I made it." And to Mary

I added, "For a while there, Jalal was the only doctor who thought I would survive."

"I'm not a doctor," was Mary's rejoinder, "but I thought you would too."

For a while we discussed business matters. I peppered them with questions, trying to get caught up on nearly a month's worth of news. But soon I brought the conversation around to a concern that had been weighing on my mind for some time. I was going to need many months to recover. Since I, as the founder of the company and its principal software designer, was likely to be out of commission for a long time, perhaps they had doubts about our future. Perhaps they were thinking of moving on. I wouldn't have faulted either one of them if they did; ours was a difficult situation.

So as soon as there was a lull in the conversation, I said, "Listen, there's something I want to ask both of you." I paused and swallowed hard.

"Go ahead," said Mary. "What is it?"

"Well," I plunged on, "please stay with the business, both of you. Don't go. I know it will be hard, but the business needs you. I need you."

There. It was out. I held my breath, waiting for their answer.

Mary looked taken aback. "I'm not going anywhere, Lewis," she said. "Believe me, that's not something you have to worry about."

Jalal, Iranian by birth, was a deep and thoughtful person, so I was not surprised when he took his time answering. "In my culture," he replied finally, "we take care of our friends." That was all, but the way he said it, with the full force of his feeling and personality, was more than enough.

Now truly I knew how lucky I was to have two such associates, who were not only such good partners but such good friends. Our meeting did not last too much longer after that. I quickly became tired, perhaps from relief and gratitude that my fears for the future of the business had been groundless.

One of the reasons I found it hard to fully accept Dr. Doherty's optimistic prognosis was that, as I confided often to Amy, "I'm afraid the other shoe is going to drop." The shock of being so suddenly struck down by encephalitis was still with me. My rational mind heard Dr. Doherty tell me over and over that I would recover, but unconsciously I still cringed in the shadow of that shock. What had happened once could happen again; that was the thought that haunted me against all reason.

A few days after Mary and Jalal's visit, Dr. Doherty was palpating my calves and thighs during a routine examination when she suddenly began pressing over and over in the same place.

Finally she stood up. "You have some edema in your left leg," she announced.

I knew what edema was—swelling. "Is that bad?"

"It might be a blood clot."

A jolt of panic swept through my body. I knew that a

blood clot in the leg was serious, sometimes life-threatening. That's why every night my calves were wrapped in uncomfortable plastic cuffs that a noisy pump inflated and deflated all night long—to prevent blood clots from forming.

Dr. Doherty went on to explain the consequences if there were a blood clot. I would have to stay in bed until it dissolved. Then I could choose between having a "filter" in my leg for the rest of my life or taking anticoagulant drugs for several months. Though she kept her tone matter-of-fact, trying not to alarm me, I was plenty alarmed. Forced to stay in bed again, I'd be weaker than ever.

"You need to go to Marin General and get an ultrasound," she said.

"Now?" I asked.

"Absolutely. Now." She turned to Amy. "Can you take him?" she asked.

"Of course," Amy replied.

"I'll call ahead. They'll have a full schedule, but I'll make sure they get you in. We need to know immediately." She rose, started to move toward the door, then turned back. "One more thing. Don't try to stand up. Stay in your wheelchair at all times."

Within minutes I was fully dressed, and Amy was rolling me down the hall in my wheelchair to the car. My mind raced. This new development had happened too suddenly for me to handle. Had the other shoe indeed dropped? Was this the moment I had been dreading? We went through the front doors and out into the sunlight, then Amy spent several minutes carefully transferring me from the wheelchair to the front seat of our car. It took her several more minutes to fold the wheelchair and stow it in the trunk.

Then we were off. Instantly, it seemed to me, we had parked at Marin General and were rolling through its hallways, up elevators, down more hallways, and into one waiting room, then another—a dizzying, confusing maze. I held my hands over my ears to dampen the whine of power saws and drills from a nearby remodeling project as we sat together in a crowded waiting room and waited to be called. Though Amy counseled me to be patient, several times I had her check at the admitting desk, and each time she returned to tell me that they knew about me, and would squeeze me in when they could. But there were several people ahead of me.

I could feel my steadily mounting anxiety beginning to spiral out of control. It must have shown on my face, because Amy reached out and put her hand on my knee.

"It's all right," she whispered. "Take it easy."

Dubiously, I nodded. Without consciously deciding to, I noticed that I was now doing the most basic of all Buddhist meditations: counting the breath. One. Two. Three. Four. I squeezed Amy's hand and closed my eyes, my chin on my chest. Stay in the moment. Don't worry about the future. Don't panic. Whatever happens. One. Two. Three. Four. The angry whine of the nearby construction equipment continued to assault my ears. One. Two. Three. Four.

"Lewis Richmond!" the attendant called out.

At last! One final shaky exhale, and Amy wheeled me into the ultrasound room, the size of a large closet, and onto the examining bed. As the technician attached the various electrodes and ran through her preliminary tests, from my prone position I asked, "Can you tell me the results as soon as you see them?"

"I'm sorry," she said pleasantly. And she pointed to a sign at the foot of the bed. I beckoned for Amy to help me put on my glasses, and with a hand over one eye, I could just read the large print: "Technicians are not permitted to discuss results of tests with patients." So I was not the first nervous nelly who couldn't wait to know. That was small comfort to my pounding heart.

Concentrating furiously, I kept counting my breaths. One. Two. Three. Four.

The technician rubbed a warm, sticky goo all over my legs and ran the sensor up and down them, pausing here and there. Why was she lingering so long on my left knee? I studied her expression for any clue, but she was inscrutable, absorbed in the click-clacking of commands into her computer.

I glanced over at Amy, sitting patiently in the corner. She gave me her most reassuring smile.

One, two, three, four.

At last the test was done.

"When will we know the answer?" I asked the technician as Amy helped me push my pants back up onto my legs.

"I'm afraid I can't say," she said in the same professional, pleasant voice. "Check with your doctor."

Well, I would certainly do that.

Then I was rolling back through the same maze of hallways, out to the car, where Amy helped me once again negotiate the difficult transfer from wheelchair to car seat. We drove in silence back to Kentfield hospital, Amy absorbed in driving, and I in my panicky thoughts.

Once we were back inside, and rolling down the hall toward my room, I had already resigned myself to a few more hours of anxious waiting when the Unit 3 nurses spied me from a distance and all started waving. "Negative, negative!" they called out.

"Negative?" I hardly dared to believe it. How did they know? When we got closer I called back, "No blood clot?"

"No," the head nurse said. "Dr. Doherty called and got the results immediately. No clot."

I sagged into my wheelchair as relief filled my whole body. It had been a false alarm. The other shoe had not dropped after all, at least not today.

The nurses all came out from behind the counter and surrounded me with laughter and congratulations. They were all so happy for me. All of them knew what I had been going through, and with all they had do in their busy day, they still kept me in their thoughts. How impressive, and how grateful I was to have a doctor that took such good care of me, and had the ability to make the bureaucracy of a large hospital generate instant results.

These people, until recently complete strangers, were

more than paid caregivers. From their myriad small acts of care, I could see that their concern for me was more than professional. They were almost like a family for me. Later that evening, as I was drifting off to sleep, I suddenly remembered one of my coma dreams, a dream about family.

I am wandering through a large garden, picking my way through rows of corn and tomatoes. The landscape seems vaguely familiar. In the distance I see an older man in a straw hat hoeing in the ground. "Hi, there," I say. "This looks like the backyard of the house I lived in as a boy."

He shades his eyes from the sun and looks me up and down. "There's nobody lives here now. Just a crew takes care of the place. If you want to talk to the boss, he's in the shed over yonder."

As I amble down a footpath to a ramshackle wooden structure with a tin roof, I recognize it as an outbuilding of my childhood home that served as a playhouse. (Some other part of my brain knows this is not true, I have never seen this place before.)

Just outside the shed I encounter a heavyset middle-aged man in dungarees. "Hey, there, young man!" he says, with an Italian accent, holding out his hand. "My name's Guido."

"I used to live here," I murmur, as the two of us enter the shadowy interior of the shed. "See," I say, pointing to some marks on the rough wood wall, "here

are my secret signs." I wander slowly about the room, touching the walls, the workbench, a rusted iron vise. "I used to make marionettes here."

"Been a long time since anybody's lived on this place. I'm just the caretaker." He pushes open a creaky door on the opposite side of the room. "Here's the cottage. Must have been a nice little hideout for someone, a long time ago."

I peer in through the doorway and see a small bedroom. It has a musty odor. It is bare of furnishings but for a torn armchair, a bed with bare mattress, a kitchen sink.

"My mom lived up here," I said, with a catch in my voice. "She and Dad didn't get along." (Again, the observer in my brain knows that none of this is true.)

"That's too bad," Guido says, shaking his head. He claps his hand on my shoulder. "Say, why don't you come down to the barn and meet the others? We were just going to have a little toast."

I follow him down another rutted path into a decrepit barn, in which ten or so men and women, all about his age, are sitting on bales of hay in a semicircle around a wooden keg set up on a sawhorse.

The people all greet me cordially as Guido produces a stack of glasses and begins to fill them, one by one, from the keg, and pass one to each of the group, and then to me. Finally he pours one for himself. I sniff the liquid. Instead of the beer I expect, it is whiskey.

Guido solemnly raises his glass. "Here's to our dear

departed friend, Roberto. We loved him like a brother,
and we'll miss him like one too."

"To Roberto!" the crowd repeats as they drink. The
whiskey is smooth, and warm to my stomach. Although
I have only been here a few moments, I already feel they
have accepted me into their family. I never had a family
like that. I never felt the warmth and care of so many
friends, so many people willing to accept me just as I am
and take me in as their own.

Here at Kentfield, this sense of family and community
was no dream. I could see it in Dr. Doherty's face, the
nurses' faces, on the walls of my room, which were plas-
tered with get-well drawings from a local Buddhist group,
and in the numerous phone calls and e-mails that Amy
brought in every day and read to me. The circle of dream
companions was mirrored in real life.

For the first time I truly appreciated the parable of the
Buddha and the mustard seed. How can we bear the suffering that each of us must endure in our lives? Because
we do not have to do so alone. Grief is strong, but gratitude is stronger. In his play *No Exit,* Jean-Paul Sartre
writes, "Hell is other people." But now I knew that this
existential aphorism was not so, at least not for me. Other
people are not hell, they are heaven, a heaven filled with
gratitude for their presence and their care.

It was on the strength of this gratitude that I was able
to gradually set aside my sorrow and self-pity and mobi-
lize the energy and determination I would need for the

long healing ahead. Soon a new phrase popped into my head, which I would repeat to myself for many weeks after: "I am strong. I am strong. I am strong."

It was not literally true. In so many ways I was profoundly weak. But perhaps, I thought, if I repeated this phrase long and sincerely enough, like Maria's daily prayer when she was bedridden for three years, it would someday come true.

And I found myself expanding on my original prayer of gratitude so that it now went:

I am grateful for my life.
I am grateful for my wife.
I am grateful for my friends.
I am grateful for my business partners.
I am grateful for this day to be alive.

SIX

DETERMINATION

As memories of the darkness fade, Lazarus, though too weak to walk, remembers how strong he once was, and how vigorous. Day by day, step by step, he determines to regain his health. One day his wife enters his chamber, carrying his morning meal, and finds him standing at the edge of the bed, his arms braced and trembling against the table nearby. Hastily setting down the tray, she goes to him and eases him back into the bed. "I can stand," he murmurs as she arranges the covers over his chest. "I can stand."

I came into Kentfield Rehabilitation Hospital with no idea what would be required of me. At first, I thought the word *rehabilitation* meant that when I left the facility, I would be fully recovered. In fact, since this was an acute care hospital, a patient leaves when he no longer needs the around-the-clock attendance of doctors and nurses (or sometimes when the insurance runs out). Full recovery might still be months or years in the future, if at all.

Once I finally understood how protracted the healing process was going to be, I wanted my time in the hospital to be over as quickly as possible. My determination was so strong, and my need for reassurance so constant, that my repeated demands for a measure of my progress at first struck Dr. Doherty as possible signs of short-term memory loss. Later cognitive tests showed only modest problems with memory, but Dr. Doherty kept reminding me, "In neurological healing, we don't think in weeks, but months."

Possibly my drive to work so hard was a legacy of my Buddhist meditation training. The hardest challenge of meditation is simply to stay at it, month after month, year after year, practicing what I often called "crawling back to the cushion." In a typical meditation retreat, it is not unusual to sit on one's cushion for ten, twelve, even sixteen hours a day. Even advanced students sometimes falter, thinking, "How can I go on? What's the point? Maybe this is enough." I can remember many times when I would loiter outside the meditation hall during a break, garnering my courage to "crawl back to the cushion," to try again.

When the Buddha himself sat down under the tree of enlightenment, he vowed, "Though only my skin and bones remain, and my blood dry up, I will not abandon this seat until I have achieved liberation." Even when Mara, the Tempter, tried to distract him with visions of hailstorms, thunderbolts, and beautiful maidens, the Buddha-to-be was unmoved, and finally he reached out to touch the earth beneath him. "Let the earth bear witness to my determination," the Buddha said, and the earth shook in acknowledgment, vanquishing Mara for good. Even today Buddha statues all over the world show the seated Buddha with his hand reaching out, in the so-called earth-touching posture.

The only connection between this inspirational story of the Buddha under a tree and I in my hospital bed was that even for me the earth shook. It was the afternoon my good friend Sylvia was visiting. As she and Amy were by my bed, chatting with me, the glass patio doors began to rattle, and soon the whole building was shaking vigorously. Was it malfunctioning machinery, a hallucination, something wrong with my bed? No, after a few moments it was clear that we were in the midst of an earthquake, a large one. I had been feeling discouraged, and had just remarked to Sylvia, "I'm trying as hard as I can, but I'm frustrated that it's taking so long to see any improvement." But once the earthquake started, though I heard the sound of shouting voices and running feet out in the hall, I suddenly felt completely calm. In my own strident determination to get better just as fast as I could, the shaking earth seemed to provide me with some confirmation, as I realized that for a few moments at least, I wasn't alone in having fallen completely apart; the whole world was with me.

So perhaps my years of crawling back to the cushion did help me find the determination I now needed. To have spent fifteen years of my life studying meditation would probably rank rather low in the ordinary person's hierarchy of modern life accomplishments. But in healing from a devastating illness, I think it was a valuable asset in helping me cope with the daily challenges of the rehabilitation process.

My Buddhist master was once asked, "Why do we practice meditation?"

He replied, "So you can enjoy your old age."

At the time we all took it as a joke, but he was serious. When we are young and healthy, we can imagine many better things to do than "crawling back to the cushion." But when we are old or sick, that experience suddenly becomes a treasure.

On the third day of my stay, while Amy and I were listening to the radio in my room, Dr. Doherty came to my room holding a small bottle and an eyedropper. "Time to test your swallowing," she announced cheerfully, and began to fill up the eyedropper with a blue fluid.

Until I could swallow without having the food or liquid go "down the wrong tube," the breathing hole in my throat could not be closed, nor could my stomach tube come out. Taking food into the lungs could cause aspiration pneumonia, with possibly deadly results.

"Open wide," she said.

I did my best to stretch my jaw open, and felt the cool, salty taste of the blue liquid as it trickled down my throat.

"Now we wait," Dr. Doherty said, capping the bottle. "I'll be back in thirty minutes to check for any blue dye coming out of your trach."

So this was my first big test. Amy held my hand while I waited, tense and expectant.

At last Dr. Doherty was back. She spent a suspenseful minute peering closely at the hole in my throat.

"No blue," she announced. "Two more in a row like that, and your trach can come out."

I couldn't wait. The thought that I might soon talk and eat made me nearly feverish with excitement, though the possibility that either of the two succeeding tests might fail, delaying the great moment for who knows how long, was its troubling counterpart, along with a secret fear that once I began to talk I would discover that something was wrong with my speech—my pronunciation, syntax, or logic.

Meanwhile, every morning I awoke to the same troubling sight: two wall clocks, two wall calendars, two doorknobs. When I held up my right hand, I saw ten fingers—no improvement since my days in the intensive care ward.

Now able to write a bit, I scrawled "DOUBLE VISION?" on a sheet of paper and showed it to Dr. Doherty the next time she visited.

"It's a common side effect of brain injury," she responded. "It will clear, but it can a take a while."

"How long?" I wrote.

"Up to six months."

My heart sank.

Seeing my crestfallen expression, she continued, "That's an outside estimate. The problem is not with your eyes. It's normal for them to send two images to the brain, which is responsible for merging them into one. Newborn babies aren't born with this ability, they have to learn it. And your brain will have to learn it again."

So the problem was in my brain. And if it had to retrain itself to see straight, I was determined to help it along. So every morning I would lie in bed and struggle mightily to merge the two clocks I saw, visualizing the two images like two ends of a giant spring that I was trying to squeeze together. Sometimes they would get a bit closer, but soon they would drift apart again. While I waited for my nurse to arrive to begin my morning routine, this became my morning meditation.

Meanwhile, my daily physical therapy was continuing. After ten days of exercises in my bed and then my wheelchair, Esther, now my principal therapist, announced, "Tomorrow we'll go to the gym."

I had seen the gym on my wheelchair tours of the hallways with Amy. It seemed like an intimidating place.

Suppose I was incontinent there? Suppose I fainted? I didn't feel ready.

Nevertheless, the next day at the appointed hour Esther wheeled me into a large room already occupied by four or five patients sitting or lying on raised mats, with one or two therapists attending each of them. The noise of all these people was loud and confusing to my hypersensitive ears. I felt as though I were in a giant echo chamber. I seem to have lost the ability to focus on any one sound to the exclusion of others, so I could barely hear Esther when she took one arm, while her assistant took the other, and said, "Put your hands here, on the armrests of your wheelchair."

I did as she instructed, and with their help and urging pushed myself up to standing, my arms trembling violently from the effort.

Once I was on my feet, she continued, "Left foot forward—a little more."

I struggled to comply.

"That's right, now turn."

She was teaching me the "transfer"—a complex minuet to move from the wheelchair to the mat. By the time I was seated, teetering on the edge of the mat, Esther and her assistant on either side holding me tight, I was breathless and sweating.

Then they had me lie down, and the real work began.

"Can you lift your leg? Good! A little more?"

I gritted my teeth, straining with all my might, and managed to lift my leg about three inches off the mat.

After a few minutes I raised my hand, signaling them that I needed to stop.

Esther peered down at my face. "You look a little pale." She turned to her assistant. "Better check his blood pressure."

Even though these twice-daily half-hour sessions were exhausting, I wanted to accomplish as much as possible. It seemed to me that if an hour of therapy was good, two or three hours should be better. Dr. Doherty explained that this was not so, at least not in my case. "Ninety percent of neurological healing, and the most important part, is done by your own brain, and only ten percent by the therapy. The therapy simply directs the brain to relearn the motor skills in the right way. The most important job for you now is to rest and heal. At a certain point more therapy becomes self-defeating."

During this time my second blue-dye test, conducted by Art, the respiratory therapist, had also been successful. After another week it was time for my third test. If I passed, I would be able to talk and eat. If I failed, I would have to start all over again. Once more it was Art who administered the test, but as he and Amy waited in the room with me for half an hour to elapse before he could check my trach, several of the nurses poked their heads in. It seemed that word had spread—I was on my third blue-dye test. Each one of them had a smile, or a thumbs-up sign, or some encouraging word. They all seemed to know how important this moment was to me.

The thirty minutes were up: time to check. Art leaned

over me and peered into my trach opening. Seconds ticked by. I held my breath. He leaned still closer. Still he said nothing.

I knew it—I had failed. I would be prisoner to a pad of paper and a stomach tube for who knew how much longer.

Just when I had resigned myself to this prospect, Art's face broke into a wide grin. "Looks like you passed!" he announced.

I lifted both my fists in triumph as high as they would go—about six inches now—and heaved a big sigh of relief.

"I'm going to cap your trach now," Art said. "Ready to start talking?"

Was I ever. He inserted a small rubber cap in my breathing hole, allowing my breath to pass over my vocal cords.

"Okay," he said. "Say something."

"Hi!" I said, and stopped short, amazed at the sound of my own voice. "Amy! Can you hear me? I can talk!"

"I can hear you," she replied, smothering me in a big hug.

"How does it feel?" Art asked.

"Wonderful!" I replied.

My voice sounded raspy and mechanical, since there was still a plastic device implanted in my throat, where it would remain for another two weeks. But I didn't care how it sounded, just that it made a sound. As Art rushed off to inform Dr. Doherty about our success, a month's worth of pent-up chatter came pouring out of my mouth. What's more, as I listened to myself talk, I suddenly realized that my fear that my language skills might be damaged was groundless. Speech therapists had visited a few times these past weeks to prepare me for possible diction problems, helping me to practice mouthing syllables— guh, duh, fruh. But all that proved unnecessary. My pronunciation, syntax, vocabulary, and logic were all normal.

Suddenly the telephone next to my bed was not just a plastic decoration—it was now my link to the outside world. I called everyone I could think of, and began every conversation the same way. "Hi! This is Lew! How do I sound?"

And the response from all my friends and associates was, "You sound great!"

Of course they couldn't see my true condition, how weak, bedridden, and impaired I truly was. As a disembodied voice on the telephone, I could nevertheless sound like my old self again. I liked that.

But inside I didn't feel anything like my old self. Aside from my physical disabilities, my sensory fog gave the world an unreal cast, as though seen through frosted glass. An ice machine in the hallway just outside my room hummed loudly all day and into the night.

"Why does it have to be so loud?" I kept asking Amy.

"What does?" Amy asked.

I had to explain. She had not noticed the sound.

The day that Andy, my lawyer, came to visit, I decided to put my sensory fog to the test.

"Andy," I said as soon as he was seated, "before we get started, there's something you need to know. I feel as though I'm on some mind-altering drug. The world looks very strange to me, and sometimes machine noises are so loud I can barely hear people talking to me." Andy, besides being my lawyer, was a good friend, one I trusted completely. I knew that whatever I asked him, he would not sugar the cookie, but be completely candid. So I took a deep breath and continued, "Can you tell? Can you see it?"

"Not at all," he replied cheerily. "You seem completely normal to me."

That was a relief. At least my strange inner world was invisible to anyone but me. Clearly I appeared more normal than I felt, and as we moved on to legal issues, I had no problem staying with the conversation. That part of my brain was fine. I was still all topsail and no keel, but at least the topsail was holding its own.

My neighbor in the next room had severe leg and brain injuries. One day I watched his therapists taking him down the hallway past my room. He was a large man, strong and powerful, but each time he pleaded with them like a frightened child. "Please let me sit down, please, please," he would plead. "No," a therapist would say. "Five more feet, then you can rest." "No, I can't do it! You have to let me rest!" "You can do it." I can only imagine the pain he must have felt, but each time, in spite of himself, he did it.

So when Dr. Doherty explained during one of her daily visits to my room that her rehabilitation philosophy was to push the patient—not beyond his limit, but all the way to it—I understood. "If you want to recover quickly, that's how," she explained.

Soon I had an opportunity to put that philosophy to the test. As Esther and her assistant were wheeling me into the gym for my daily therapy, while Amy waited for me in my room, Esther announced that it was time for me to try standing on my own, without their support.

No, I thought. I wasn't strong enough. It was beyond my limit. Nevertheless, she wheeled me up to a ladderlike structure built into one wall of the gym and the two of them lifted me to my feet.

"Go ahead," Esther said as they shifted their hands to hold my chest. "Grab on to the highest rung you can."

I reached out with first one hand, then the other, and clutched a rung at chest height.

"Higher," she demanded. "You can go higher."

One rung higher, then two. My shoulders ached from the strain. They let go of me; I was on my own now. Esther started a stopwatch, while her assistant expanded and contracted the blood pressure cuff on my arm.

"Thirty seconds." Esther called out. "Keep it up!" My legs were already trembling violently, but remembering my neighbor with the bad leg, pleading for mercy in the hallway, I hung on for dear life. "One minute!" My knees were buckling. "How's his pressure?" "Ninety over sixty." Borderline. "Ninety seconds!" I couldn't go on.

"Do you want to sit down?" Esther asked, seeing my face gone pale.

I shook my head.

"Two minutes. Try for thirty more seconds."

I counted them under my breath, one thousand one, one thousand two. The longest half-minute of my life. Then I collapsed back into my chair, panting and dizzy. But I had done it.

"Great job," Esther congratulated me.

After the session was over, as Esther wheeled me into my room, I was triumphant. "I stood," I told Amy, who put down her magazine as I came in. "Two minutes thirty seconds."

"I know," she said, with a secret smile. "I saw you. I was watching you the whole time from just outside the gym."

I don't know who was happier, she or I. That afternoon she went out and bought some chocolate tofutti for us to eat together in celebration. The silky texture of that confection, and the richness of the chocolate, were a fitting reward for all my hard work, and when my spoon scraped the bottom of the plastic container, I wished she had bought two.

Within days Esther had graduated me from standing to walking, using the parallel bars, which intimidated me even more than standing. The evening of my first day on the parallel bars, while a blond nurse's aide named Victor was helping me prepare for bed that night, I told him how frightened I was trying to walk on this new apparatus.

"There's a mirror at the end of the walkway," I said. "So I can see myself try to walk. I had no idea how awful I looked." It was true. I looked like a bearded scarecrow, holding onto the parallel bars for dear life, terrified I might fall.

I already knew how strong Victor was. He could lift my body up off the bed unaided, even though he was only about five foot seven. Now he explained why: he had been a wrestler, and had trained hard for many years. His only reaction to my tale of woe were the softly spoken words, "No fear."

Then he explained in simple but eloquent English how his wrestling training had taught him that valuable lesson. "One time I was visiting this friend of mine at a store where he worked. He needed to go across the street to buy something, and asked me to mind the store while he was gone. And as soon as he left, this guy came in, pulled a knife, and asked for all the money.

"So before he could move or do anything, I leaped over the counter and twisted the knife out of his hand and threw him down on the floor. Then I held him there with a wrestling hold while I grabbed the phone with the other hand and called the police. Boy, when my friend came back, was he surprised!"

"Weren't you afraid?" I asked, deeply impressed by his story.

"No," he replied. "No fear."

Perhaps it was my reaction to the story or the lateness of the hour, but the moment he finished telling his tale, I suddenly needed to go to the bathroom. Ordinarily Victor would have to roll in a special chair from the bathroom, position it next to my bed, help me sit on it, and wheel me back into the bathroom. But this time he shook his head and pointed to the bathroom door. "You can walk," he said in a voice that was suddenly commanding and firm.

"No, no!" I protested. "I can't walk. I'm too weak. You have to hold me."

"No fear," he said, softly, as he helped me sit up and then stand. "No fear."

I took first one step, then another. I teetered, but didn't fall over. Victor was by my side, his hand ready if I should stumble, but as I shuffled the five or six steps into the bathroom, he didn't need to touch me. I made it by myself. As I sat down on the toilet, both of us grinned at each other.

No fear.

The next day, I mounted the parallel bars and surprised myself as well as Esther by walking the length of the ramp only needing to grab the bars twice.

Once again, one of the nurses had become my teacher.

Encouraged by my success in the gym, I was now more determined than ever to teach my brain to see one clock. Dr. Doherty didn't think that any amount of conscious effort could hasten the process. But I wanted to try anyway.

It was about three weeks of daily effort before I began to notice the first tiny change: when Amy sat next to my bed, three or four feet away, I could sometimes—only sometimes—resolve her image into one face.

"One face," I would say to her, pointing. "One face."

But as soon as I spoke, the single image would separate into two again. "Damn!"

Strangely enough, at first this phenomenon didn't seem to work for any other objects or faces. Then it occurred to me that a baby's first image, and the one she values most, is her mother's face. Dr. Doherty had said my brain had to relearn vision the way a baby does. Perhaps that's what my brain was starting to do. I couldn't think of any other explanation. There was a special magic for me in knowing that alone of all the people in the hospital, the face I loved most was the one I could see best. As frustrating as my effort to see straight was, the poignancy of this fact was most encouraging to me.

Over the next several days there was further improvement. Now when Dr. Doherty stood at the foot of her bed with her clipboard, I could say, "I see just one face, doctor."

She was surprised and pleased at my quick progress. And one memorable day I woke up and saw just one clock. At last I could tell the time without having to cover one eye. Regardless of whether my efforts had hastened the relearning process, or whether it was destined to happen quickly anyway, that moment was a real triumph for me.

Though I was meeting the hospital's therapeutic goals for me more quickly than Dr. Doherty had expected, I had my own private goals as well. Could I still type? Could I play the piano? Both were important to me, especially the piano. Music had been at the center of my life since I was six years old—my first love, my source of inspiration, my passion—the medium that most allowed me to express my deep feeling. Suppose I were to finally sit down at a piano and find that this lifelong skill was gone, perhaps permanently? I would be devastated.

Dr. Doherty had told me on the first day that there was a piano somewhere in the hospital building, but for quite a while I was afraid to ask where. Instead I "played" the piano on my bedsheets, using "Mothers," the first piece on my solo piano album, as my model, trying to hear the music in my head as I performed the finger movements on my chest. Technically it was an easy piece. If I could still play anything with my oven-mitt fingers, this would be it. I was also testing my musical memory, once so formidable. At first I had a hard time remembering, but little by little it came back to me. What a fine feeling, the day I "played" the piece all the way through! One more piece of my brain that still seemed to be working. But how well would my clumsy fingers function on a real keyboard?

Each morning when I awoke, my first thought was, Is this the day? Will I finally get up the nerve to ask Amy to take me to the piano? But the day would pass without my asking.

I might have procrastinated indefinitely, but one day the decision was made for me. Katherine, my recreational therapist, was a bright, enthusiastic young woman whose job it was to keep me occupied and entertained. On her first day with me she arrived in my room with a deck of cards and some board games. That day and over time I made an effort to try these diversions, but for various reasons I found them difficult. The Monopoly pieces were too small for my clumsy fingers. Card games required too much sustained concentration. In any case, games had never been a part of my life before my illness. I much preferred to pass my spare time lying quietly in bed.

But Katherine was determined to find something to lift my spirits. That, after all, was her job.

"All right," she said finally. "What would you really like to do?"

Without thinking I blurted out, "Play the piano!"

"Well, then, let's go!" she said brightly. I glanced over at Amy, who was with us in the room, and started to protest that it was still too soon, I was not ready, but Katherine had already moved to the back of my wheelchair, ready to wheel me off to the hospital's recreation room. Soon I was rolling down the hall, Katherine behind me and Amy alongside, to a room near the hospital kitchen—sparsely furnished, empty of people, and cold. As we entered I saw, off in the corner, a spinet-size piano. Katherine slid the piano bench aside, wheeled me up to the instrument, and removed the wheelchair's footrests so I could touch the piano's pedals with my feet. I put my foot on the pedal, but I had a hard time controlling my ankle muscles. My foot kept slipping off.

I looked down at the piano keyboard, lifted my hands, and pressed a few keys. The sound clanged in my ears, tinny and too loud. I drew back.

Amy and Katherine, seated expectantly on the couch, waited to see what I would do next.

What I wanted to do was leave, go back to the safety of my room, not meet this challenge today, but instead I found myself trying a few simple finger exercises. My fingers felt clumsy and swollen, but at least I was getting around on the keys. So far it hadn't been a complete disaster.

Now for a real piece. I set my fingers over the keys of the first chord of "Mothers," and began to play.

The piece begins with a few simple chords, and continues with an even simpler melody. I wrote it as an ode to my two mothers: Arista, my biological mother who died when I was four, and Bernice, my stepmother and the woman who raised me. The whole theme of *Lake of No Shore*, my solo piano CD, is mother's love. That is why this piece is first on the album, and why, even before this illness, it was always a deeply emotional experience for me to perform it.

Now I could not play more than the first few bars before I broke down in tears and had to stop. Amy came over and held me as my shoulders heaved. The music always evoked so many sad memories for me, but this time I was crying not just from sadness but from relief.

I could still play. Not well, not at all well, but much better than I had feared. The important thing was: I could still make music. Music, my lifelong friend and soul mate, was still with me. With Amy still holding me, I started the piece over again, this time letting the music— *my* music—have its full reign of deep feeling and familiar sound.

After that first day I had vowed that however stunted my playing skill, I would try to play a little every day, and that is how I spent my daily half hour with Katherine—at the piano. And doing so had an unexpected side benefit. Dr. Doherty had said that most neurological healing is measured in months, but the dexterity needed for piano playing is so subtle that a pianist can feel the tiniest change. And every day my fingers were telegraphing tiny improvements in my healing that could not be measured any other way, a daily message that gave me great comfort and encouragement.

One day, nurse Josephine casually mentioned that Amy and I could request a "pass" to leave the hospital temporarily. I was pleased and excited by the prospect. The boredom of day-to-day hospital life was beginning to weigh on me. So with Dr. Doherty's written permission and blessing ("Go have fun!" she said), the very next Saturday I was once again in the passenger seat of our car, my wheelchair stowed in the trunk. We weren't sure where we wanted to go, just Out.

So familiar, this car, the smell of the leather upholstery, the contour of the seat, the slant of the steering wheel. I ran my hand over the controls, opened and closed the air-conditioning vents. I wished I could be in the driver's seat, to hold the gearshift, work the pedals, as I used to do. All in good time, I thought. Amy slammed the trunk lid shut, slid in behind the wheel, started the car, and we were off.

I was hoping to enjoy the drive, but the speed and the noise were disorienting. It felt as though my nose were pressed against a giant television set tuned to maximum volume. And as we rounded each curve, I found myself cringing at the approach of every oncoming car, feeling certain that it was headed directly at us. Our route took us along streets that I had driven for years, but I found them hardly recognizable. Was that our neighborhood drug-store? It looked completely unfamiliar.

When we set off, we had no particular destination in mind, just the thought of being out in the fresh air, away from the hospital. But as we drew closer to Mill Valley, where we had our home and I my office, I said, "Let's go to the office."

At first Amy was dubious. "What can you do there?" On a Saturday, it would be empty.

"I just want to see it," I replied, and attempted a joke. "Make sure it's still there."

Yes, it was there, my office building next to a placid lagoon where egrets nested. I looked up and spied the third-floor window, its blinds drawn—my private office.

"See," I said, pointing, "there it is." I was uncommonly pleased to see it there. For a moment my persona as dis-abled hospital patient dropped away, and I felt some inti-mation of a healthy self I had all but forgotten.

Presently I was reinstalled in my wheelchair and ready to enter the building. Amy held out my key ring so I could show her which one opened the outside door. The eleva-tor sounded and smelled so familiar as we rode up. And a few moments later she held open the office door while I rolled through it, reached up to switch on the light, and surveyed the space. It looked both familiar and strange, two opposing sensations. I rushed around in my wheel-chair like a kid in a candy store, exploring each drawer of my desk, fumbling with keys and unlocking cabinets. Suddenly realizing that I could copy an e-mail program from my office computer to the laptop back at the hospital and begin e-mailing my friends, I flicked on the machine, inserted a diskette, and tapped out some complicated instructions, delighted to discover that I could still remember how to do this. I stuffed the diskette in my jacket pocket, another portal to the world now accessible to me. When we left, I made smiley-face signs and put them on my partners' desks, with the message, "I was here—Lewis."

I sat for a few more moments in my comfortable office chair, looking out the window at the rippling waves of the lagoon. The tide was going out. A few shorebirds glided lazily over the water, eyeing a possible meal—a scene I had once contemplated every day.

With a sigh, I swiveled my chair around. "Time to go, I guess," I said.

As we locked up and headed toward the elevator, Amy asked, "Can you think of anyplace else you'd like to go?"

My eyes lit up. "Let's go to the house," I said.

"All right," she said. "But remember, you can't go in." There was an outside stairway up to our front door, and at this point in my therapy I was just beginning to practice walking with the parallel bars. She was right. I could not go up those stairs and inside.

"Let's go anyway," I said. "Let me just see it." All of a sudden, I *had* to see it, just as I had the office, to reassure myself that my former dwelling place was still there, waiting for me.

Our home was a short drive from the office, through a wooded residential area and up a winding road. Amy gunned the car up our steep driveway, and there it was, our house. My home. In my haste I tried to open the passenger door by myself, but I couldn't. Amy had to do it. I reached up to brace myself against the top of the car door and pulled myself up. There I stood, inches from the exterior wall of the house that represented a now-inaccessible world to which I might soon return.

"I want to touch the wall," I said to Amy. I inched farther away from the car, still supporting myself with the door on one side while she held my elbow on the other, until I could just reach out and touch the wall with one hand. I felt an electric jolt—the rough texture of cold stucco under my hand. On the other side of this windowless wall was our garage. The living quarters were one floor up and out of sight. I couldn't see in, only touch.

I stayed in that awkward position for a long time, my head bowed, my knees shivering with effort, communing by touch with this dwelling place that was so close yet still so far. Hello, house. Hello, life, I thought. How desperately I want to return to you, and feel the familiar rug, sit on my familiar chair, sleep in my familiar bed.

But I couldn't. I couldn't, and after too long a time of standing there, my hand on the wall and my head bowed,

I slid back into the car, Amy backed slowly down the driveway into the street, and we drove back to the hospital the way we came, in silence. I shed no more tears; this day had already wrung me dry. All too soon we were back at the hospital, where Amy wheeled me down the hall to my tiny dark room and I collapsed, exhausted, into bed.

My Buddhist teacher Shunryu Suzuki used to talk frequently about effort in Buddhist practice.

"If your effort is based on some goal," he would say, "then it is good, but not good enough. If you do not meet your goal, you may become discouraged. And even if you do, you may give up your effort as no longer necessary. True spiritual effort is just to practice Zen, for its own sake, without any thought of a goal."

In healing from this illness, I needed a goal, and my determination to achieve it kept me going. But as I was soon to realize—and not for the first time in my life—Suzuki's warning about the limitation of goal-seeking effort was all too true. Fifteen years before, when I had cancer, I had to endure a full year of intense chemotherapy and radiation. During that long ordeal, I kept myself from becoming discouraged by setting a goal—a date in the future—and telling myself, Only six more months to go, five more months to go. But when my treatment was over at last, I felt not celebration but only a new sense of foreboding. I had realized, with a sinking feeling, that the doctors had done all they could for me, and there was nothing for me to do but wait—and wait—to see if I would live or die.

I was to have a similar experience when I left Kentfield. But until that day came, all I could think about as the weeks passed and the physical therapy became more grueling was the gritty feel of that stucco wall the day we visited our house, and those stairs leading up to the front door. That was my goal. Amy knew now much I yearned for the moment when I could climb those stairs and go inside, so every night, as she kissed me good-bye and prepared to leave me, her last words to me were always, "One day closer to coming home."

SEVEN

THE CURSE OF TIME

Lazarus spends most of each day in bed, as his wife and daughters tend him and care for his every need. Occasionally he sits on the balcony overlooking his garden, where he once spent hours tending his blossoms and fruit trees. Once his days were filled with prayer, and meeting with his many students. Once he enjoyed solitude as the state where man is closest to God. But now time weighs heavy on his soul, and when he is alone in bed, his mind is filled with foreboding. Time, once his ally, has now become his oppressor.

How often we desire something so powerfully that we bend all our thoughts to it, day and night, until it consumes us. And how often, when our wish finally comes true, the satisfaction that we imagined recedes like a mirage in the desert.

The Buddhists say that this process of grasping and clinging is the root of all suffering. It is also human nature, which even the wisest of us cannot entirely escape. The ideal of the early Buddhists was the world-renouncing monk—a person without possessions, ambition, or aspirations of any kind except for the highest wisdom. Later forms of Buddhism taught that the goal was not to literally eliminate all desire but to become fully aware of the process by which it rules us—an awareness that can set us free, even while living in the midst of it.

Those paragraphs might have come straight from one of my lectures when I was active as a Buddhist priest, and when I thought that my understanding of this fundamental teaching was good. But it is one thing to meditate and teach about desire. It is quite another to be swept up into the clouds by it and come crashing to earth at the very moment of its consummation.

After seven weeks at Kentfield, my single burning desire was to go home. I thought about it day and night, imagining how wonderful it would be to sleep in my own bed, to eat my own food, to live once again as a person, not a hospital patient. What I was to discover in going home was a host of unexpected new problems, the most difficult of which was a strange distortion in my sense of time.

However, on the day of my departure from Kentfield Rehabilitation Hospital, that struggle still lay in the future. As the appointed day, September 17, approached— a date sooner by half than Dr. Doherty had originally expected—I still felt only excitement and anticipation. I had come such a long way. I could now walk for short distances unaided, even at last climb stairs. I could dress myself, shower, eat, and use the bathroom—the basics of self-sufficiency.

But even toward the end, the therapists pushed me to do more. Two days before I was to leave, as I practiced walking in the hall with Esther, she suddenly said, "Let's run." One last challenge to do something I thought was beyond me. But with her hand resting lightly on my arm, she was already starting to jog and urging me to follow. I tried. My balance and coordination were still poor, my body still weak. Each time my toes touched the hallway rug, my ankles wobbled like spinning tops about to fall, and as the upper part of my body leaned forward in the natural posture of running, it felt as though it were about to separate itself from my legs. But for about thirty feet I did it, and afterward rushed back to my room to call Amy on her cell phone to tell her the news—"Today I actually ran."

The morning of my departure I awakened before dawn as excited as any kid on Christmas Day. I lay there in the dark, reviewing the triumphs and frustrations of the past seven weeks. As it grew light, for the first time I opened the sliding glass door next to my bed and ventured out into the stone courtyard beyond—a fitting symbol, I thought, for my homecoming and the new territory I was about to explore. But the early morning air was chilly, so I soon went back inside to tour all the hallways. Until recently I had only been allowed to walk in the hall just outside my room, but now I was free to explore anywhere I liked.

The long wait was over. By lunchtime I would be in my own home again. Amy had already taken home most of my clothes and other paraphernalia over the past several days. Only one duffel bag was left, to carry my toiletries and few remaining articles of clothing.

After Amy arrived, about eighty-thirty, we busied our-selves with packing and other last-minute details. One final interview with Dr. Doherty, and we could go, but the nurses said she was not due until eleven o'clock. So we waited, sitting in comfortable silence as we had done so often these past weeks—but this time it was different. This time we were going home.

Shortly after eleven Dr. Doherty arrived, had us fill out some paperwork, and handed me a bag of take-home pre-scriptions. She was effusive and happy. She didn't often have an opportunity to send one of her neurological patients home to what she anticipated would be a rosy future. And as her final healing act, she opened her arms and enveloped me in a hug. "Some great strength has seen you through this," she said. "Good luck to you. I know you'll be fine."

Suddenly she was not the all-knowing physician but a warm, caring human being, enfolding me in her embrace. My eyes watered, and I tried to think of something to say, but all I could do was look into her face and see my deep feeling mirrored in hers. I had come to have a deep affection for her during these difficult seven weeks. She was an extraordinary physician and person, a fact I did not fully appreciate until, while I was writing this book, she responded to some questions of mine with a handwritten letter:

I have the greatest job in the world—I help people to get better. Though the work, to be done right, is labor-intensive, the rewards are phenomenal. It's not just mending bodies. It's guiding patients through a process of healing body, mind, soul and putting families back together after catastrophic neurological insults.

So, after our final good-bye to Dr. Doherty, Amy and I walked down the hallway for the last time, she clutching the duffel bag and I my cane, waving good-bye to the day nursing staff, who were all smiles. I had arrived immobile, and was now walking out on my own two feet. This is what they worked for; this was why they were here.

"Come back and visit us," one of them called, and I said I would.

Then we were in the car, the noise of the wind and the engine too loud, the sunlight painfully bright, but for once I did not care. I felt as though I had scaled the tallest mountain. All that remained was to climb those twenty steps to the front door of our house and walk inside.

When we came to a stop in our driveway, I was first out of the car, teetering on the uneven asphalt of the driveway and supporting myself with one hand against the side of the house while the other clutched my cane. At last I was climbing those final steps. I counted them—one, two, three, four, up to twenty, until I was at the door. But I didn't have my keys or wallet—still a man with no identity. I waited while Amy came up behind me and opened the door for me. I hesitantly entered, felt the familiar rug soft beneath my feet, smelled the nearly forgotten house smells, saw all the familiar furniture, and immediately burst into tears. One of my therapists had warned me that homecoming day was always emotional, but I was still surprised at the intensity of it. I hobbled to the couch. It looked so odd and foreign after all this time, as I collapsed into it.

I was home at last.

It was a few days before my elation began to subside. I had spent the last two months confined to one tiny room, with nothing to do except to attend my therapy sessions, play a little piano, and take short walks. All my attention had been focused on narrow goals—how to walk, talk, use the bathroom, eat. All day I was surrounded by people encouraging me and cheering me on.

Now I was back in the real world, in my own house, huge in comparison to my hospital room, surrounded by all the artifacts of my former life—my books, my furniture, my computers, my records, a lifetime of original manuscripts—a stranger in the midst of my own world.

What's more, I was much weaker than I had realized. In the hospital my rapid daily progress had given me the illusion that I was becoming strong. But that was only in comparison to my initial condition. Now my standard of comparison was my condition before the illness, and I quickly realized that though my physical rehabilitation had gone remarkably well in its own terms, on the long road to full recovery I had a long way to go.

Then there was the reality of my mental condition. In the hospital I talked and typed a bit, but except for some cognitive testing early on, and some logical puzzles to practice, the emphasis of the rehabilitation was primarily physical. Few demands were placed on me mentally.

Late in the afternoon of my homecoming day I sat in my book-lined office and surveyed the room, cluttered with paintings, statues, two computers, and mementos. Everything shimmered with an incandescent and unreal glow. I picked a book off the shelf at random and opened to the first page. The letters swam in my vision—too bright, too sharp. In the hospital my only reading was a minute or two of the morning newspaper. Now I wanted to see how long I could go, but it was only a couple of pages before the words blurred and a strange sensation took hold in my brain. My mind simply could not process any more words on the page.

I slammed the book shut. I had no idea it was going to be like this. It seemed I couldn't do anything. More than that, I realized that although it felt as though I had been sitting in my office chair for an hour, when I glanced at my watch, only a few minutes had passed. Something was amiss with time itself. Before I was ill, I never noticed time, any more than I noticed the air I breathed. But now it had become oppressive, a harsh weight on my shoulders.

It was only later that I remembered the blurring sensation in my brain as "saturation." During the cognitive tests I had been given at the hospital, there were times when I had the same sensation and needed to stop. "You're saturated," the neuropsychologist who was testing me would say.

"What's saturated?" I asked.

A damaged brain is like a damaged muscle, he explained. Being weak, it tires easily. "Once you're saturated, you have to rest your brain for an hour or two."

The sensation I had felt when I tried to read at home was the same, the mental analog of physical exhaustion. Under the strain of real concentration, the engine of my mind had faltered and, like a stubborn mule, refused to go a step further.

Now I understood. Though my cognitive abilities were relatively intact, my attention span was not. In the face of real-life mental tasks, my brain could only function for five, at most ten, minutes before grinding to a halt. This was an unexpected and unwelcome setback.

In the face of this discouragement, I had to remind myself how far I had come, and what I *could* do. I could walk without a cane, at least inside the house. I could talk coherently on the telephone for short periods. I could ride in the car to various appointments—outpatient physical therapy at Kentfield, psychotherapy with Diane. All that certainly counted for something, but it was not nearly what I had hoped or expected.

My first effort to combat this sense of helplessness was to establish a routine, as Dr. Doherty had suggested when I left. I made up a schedule of activities to do each day, beginning with some physical exercise, typing into my journal, a little piano playing, reading (read one page, rest five minutes), a few minutes of computer programming, a half-hour walk around the neighboring streets.

I even tried a bit of Buddhist meditation, thinking that would be sure to calm me. But I quickly discovered that it felt radically different than before. As soon as I sat down on my cushion and crossed my legs, I became physically disoriented. I hardly knew up from down. My body felt scattered, like loose pieces of a jigsaw puzzle. And though I could find my breathing, it seemed disconnected from the rest of my body. Usually in the first few minutes of meditation the breath slows and deepens, and mind and body become calm. But instead my breath quickened, jittery and out of control like a loose sail flapping in the wind. And my mind buzzed and crackled—not with thoughts but with some kind of neurological noise.

As I looked up in discouragement from this long-familiar spiritual practice gone sour, my eyes spotted the beautiful statue on my altar of Amida Buddha, the Buddha of Salvation. Reaching out to take a Buddhist rosary in my hands, I kept my gaze fixed on the statue as I chanted, "Amida Buddha please protect me, Amida Buddha please protect me." This practice, for the few minutes I could stay with it, gave me some relief and comfort.

I might have been less discouraged had I remembered a comment Shunryu Suzuki once made during a lecture: "Sometimes even meditation doesn't help. Sometimes nothing helps."

I soon discovered that I could not follow the rest of my ambitious daily schedule, either. I had neither the attention span nor the energy. Even my Steinway grand piano, once my fondest love, was a disappointment. After my weeks of practice in the hospital recreation room, I could still play only the most elementary tunes, and the much bigger sound of the grand piano was harsh and unpleasant to my ears.

Each morning I awoke and glanced at the clock: 5:00 A.M. How could it be so early? How was I going to get through the day? The hours crawled so slowly. I spent much of the time sitting on the couch, waiting for the next meal or appointment, all too aware of the clock ticking next to me on the side table. And my sojourn on the couch was not just boredom. I was often too tired to do much else, having gotten so little sleep the night before.

My doctors had warned me that sleep was among the many bodily functions that would be disturbed by my brain stem injury. In fact, during the last few weeks of my stay at Kentfield, I had increasing difficulty falling asleep, and I was now dependent on a cocktail of sleeping pills. Even when I did sleep, it did not feel normal or restful. It was more like a period of uneasy blankness from which I awoke as tired as I began.

One night, after taking as many pills as I was allowed, I lay in bed wide-eyed for hours as though I had just drunk several cups of coffee. About 1:00 A.M. I got up in a panic, ran into the bathroom to splash water on my face, and woke Amy. As she put on her robe and came to me, I fell to my knees, clutching her legs, and started to wail—an unearthly cry from deep in my belly. "I can't go on like this!" I cried. "I can't sleep. I'll never sleep!" I felt that I was losing all control, in the grip of some deeper, more elemental force that was tearing me apart.

Amy held me as I buried my head in her stomach and sobbed. It took a while, but at last her soothing words and comforting touch finally calmed me, and after she encouraged me to take another tranquilizer, I returned to bed and sank into a few hours' troubled sleep.

When morning came, I was calmer. The events of the previous night were now relegated to that alcove of memory reserved for nightmares. Nevertheless, I placed an urgent call to my family doctor, Dr. Belknap. A good friend as well as an excellent doctor (it was he who had discovered my cancer, fifteen years before, by pursuing symptoms that most doctors would have dismissed as trivial), he launched into action. After a conference call with my other doctors, he recommended a new combination of sleeping drugs, designed to cope with my intractable insomnia. I was now dreading bedtime and what new terrors the night might bring, but over the next few days these new drugs prevented any repetition of my earlier nightmare, and my dire fantasies about being forevermore sleepless began to fade. It was sobering and unsettling, though, to realize that my condition was so fragile that at any time I could be surprised with such a sudden deterioration.

And that was only one of many worries that haunted my days. As I discussed these with Diane during our therapy sessions, we narrowed them down to what I called "the three terrors"—fear that something terrible might happen to Amy, or to me, or to my business. The fact that so far the business was doing just fine without me did nothing to assuage this last fear.

Diane recognized these fears as "catastrophic thinking," and said it was not unusual after a great shock or trauma. "Of course," she explained, "any of those things might happen, to you or to me or to anyone, but we can't live our lives in fear of them. We all must develop an assumption of safety that allows us to get through the day. I have three children, and if I allowed myself to worry constantly that one of them might be hit by a car, or could be kidnapped, I wouldn't be able to function."

"I know." I nodded miserably as we sat together in her

office, she in a chair and I on the couch, wearing sunglasses to protect myself from the brightness of my sensory fog, which still showed no signs of subsiding. "I know. But I can't stop myself. These thoughts just rise up and hound me, all day long. And they seem so real."

I could also see, from my Buddhist training, that I was having to confront the fundamental truth of the universe—everything changes, nothing lasts, disaster can strike at any time—with a brain that lacked the strength to cope with it. Despite all my years of meditation, and all my efforts to live my life in accordance with this truth, I was now grasping for its opposite, for permanence, for safety, for the hope that nothing else would go wrong.

"I'm like a frightened child," I admitted to Diane. "And I can't seem to do anything about it."

"Yes," Diane agreed. "The trauma of the disease, and the damage it caused your brain, has made you like a child in certain ways. But it won't last. Besides, these terrors are not that irrational, only your measure of them. You just need to make them munchkins rather than monsters. All your doctors have told you that you will get better. You need to focus on that."

"How?" That future promise seemed so weak compared to the power of my present troubles.

"Try to visualize wellness. Try to picture yourself as you will be in a month. What do you see?"

In a month I would have my follow-up appointment with Dr. Doherty.

I closed my eyes and tried to visualize that meeting. "In

a month," I said, "when I see Dr. Doherty, my vision and hearing will be better, my herky-jerky walking will be smoother, and I will be actively involved with my business."

"Good!" Diane replied approvingly. "And how do you see yourself when you are completely well?"

Completely well? Would there ever come such a time? Nevertheless, I immediately imagined myself in a white turtleneck, wearing my favorite leather jacket, hiking with Amy down the steep hill from our house and all the way up again, strong and unaided.

"Wonderful," she exclaimed. "Whenever those terrors come up, try to concentrate on those positive visions, because that is what is actually going to happen, not your imagined catastrophes."

For the next week I tried Diane's advice, and found that these healing images did give me some solace. And I didn't stop there; as I lay in bed each morning, I tried to visualize some other images that would give me strength. The first image that swam into view was of Arista, my biological mother, who died when I was barely four, whose face I knew not from memory but only from photographs. From her I felt unconditional love. Over the next few days she was joined by a shadowy robed figure who gradually took the form of my Buddhist teacher, Shunryu Suzuki, his face placid and neutral, deep in meditation. It was another week before a third image joined them: first a heavily muscled arm, then a power- fully built young man in a T-shirt, sleeves rolled up. I called him Butch.

"Those are wonderful images," Diane said when I told her about them. "Pay attention to what they might say or do. They are projections of your own unconscious, trying to help you."

The images did not say or do much, and the one of Suzuki never spoke at all. It was more their various attitudes that helped me. Butch was tough and strong, and often appeared to me with his fist upraised, his bicep bulging. My mother glowed with constant warmth and love. And Suzuki just sat there, doing nothing, saying nothing, reminding me that I could draw strength from the spiritual tradition and practices he had taught me.

Once, while I was lying in bed, early in the morning, visualizing these figures, Butch did speak to me, and this is what he said:

Hey!
This is a journey.
The journey is a river.
The river is long.
Follow the river.

And then he clenched his fist.

On October 5 I visited my neurologist, Dr. Castleman, who offered a more medical perspective on my problems. He was delighted to see me, and thrilled at my progress. He was one of the doctors who had attended me in the coma. It was he who had first told Amy how grim my condition was.

But as I sat in his office with Amy, he was all smiles. "It's unbelievable," he said, hearing me describe all that I could do.

"Computer programming?" he repeated in disbelief.

"Yes," I replied. "About ten minutes a day." Like reading, this was a skill I could manage, though not for long.

"And you do it well?"

"I think so," I said.

He shook his head. "Most people recovering from a case of encephalitis as serious as yours just sit staring off into space while their family talks for them. You're in miracle territory."

"What were my odds, do you think?" I asked. "A hundred to one?"

"No." He shook his head. "I would say a thousand to one."

Then the discussion turned to the symptoms that most disturbed me—the fog, my limited attention span, my insomnia at night and anxiety during the day.

"The brain heals very slowly," he explained. "Especially your inhibitory functions. More than half of the brain is devoted to inhibiting the activity of the other half," he explained. "Sleep, for example, inhibits wakefulness. Calm inhibits anxiety. Your whole brain swelled during the illness, your spinal cord too. You need to give them time to settle down and heal."

In my present state of mind, patience was most difficult, but over the next couple of weeks I did begin to notice one welcome improvement—to my sensory fog. It was hard to sense the change inside the house, where sights and sounds were muted, but at the supermarket, with the rumble of refrigeration equipment and bright colors on the shelves, I noticed that the fog was at last beginning to subside.

That was a most welcome development, but it did not assuage the isolation and loneliness that my illness had forced on both Amy and myself. Once, driving home from the store, we saw a homeless couple holding a sign hand-lettered on cardboard, "Family Stranded." I felt a wave of sadness well up in my chest. When I glanced over at Amy behind the wheel, I saw the tears on her cheeks too. I had my therapies and my appointments, but most of the time it was just the two of us, alone together in the house, sitting across from each other at the kitchen table. I knew from looking in the mirror that my face appeared haunted, perhaps even a bit deranged, and I would apologize to her every day for not being able to better control my fears. From across the table she would cradle my hands in hers and do her best to comfort me, but neither she nor I had any real idea how to deal with the day-to-day trial of my condition.

One evening, as Amy was standing next to me at the dinner table, I suddenly put my arms around her waist, buried my head in her stomach, and began to weep uncontrollably. "I wish it hadn't happened!" I cried out. "I want our life back. I want things to be the way they were before."

She started to cry too. "I know," she said, stroking my

hair, "I know." And we remained there for what seemed like a long, long, time, sharing our grief.

Now finally I had seen her grief, which she had kept hidden to avoid upsetting me further. Now I understood the toll my condition was taking on her too. I felt ashamed for always concentrating on myself. From that day forward I vowed not to burden her so much with my problems. I wrote it down in my journal: "I must be more considerate of Amy's feelings." Every day I tried, but every day I felt that I had failed.

Most of my journal entries during this time were short and perfunctory. I couldn't muster the energy for much more, and my customary facility with words seemed to have left me. Occasionally, though, moments of creativity broke through:

I guess you might say I'm just a naked young cuss because I haven't got hardly a hair on me. Naked as a jaybird they say except I'm no jaybird but a walking, talking, grown-up man who's had the stuffing kicked out of him all of a sudden and stuck with what's left. They say I'll have it all back someday, that empty bag will fill up and I'll be whole, but try telling an empty sack of potatoes that someday, some by-and-by, it'll be full to the brim with ripe new fruit. On the other hand, you watch a potato grow and you realize that making a potato ain't no overnight matter. You got to sow, and water, and weed, and hoe, all the while that little tuber is doing its work under the ground so that one day it can poke up and see a bit of sun. And it takes quite a while after that before anything like a potato starts to show itself, and even then it's all underground, where you have to dig and mess up the growing process to even see it.

That's how it is with potatoes, and I reckon it's not much different for a man, except a man has his memories and pride, and his reputation and future, and can't be expected to be as passive and patient as a potato. How does a man all of a sudden turn himself into a potato gestating in the soil and sun? That's the question, and if you have any hint of an answer don't hesitate to shout it out, because over here in potato-man land, we're fresh out of answers, though we are cultivating a bit of patience on the side. It suffices for now, though patience is no vegetable and comes and goes pretty much as it pleases.

One afternoon in late October I was lying outside on a lounge chair watching the undulating branches of the small forest of pine trees on the hillside above me. Scenes of nature often soothed me. These trees are my friends, I told myself, they help me. For a while my attention melted into the texture of the foliage, as I reflected on how a tree passes the time—slowly, deliberately, imperceptibly. Some of the pine needles were greener than others—fresh new growth, just as there was inside my brain. I studied a patch of dead branches and thought, "Yes, that's me.

When the time is right, the sick part will fall away and the new growth will come." But it will take time, time, so much time.

Time! Suddenly I was frightened. "Amy!" I cried out in a tone that made her come running. "I can't live like this. There's nothing I can do! I can't read, I can't watch television, I can't play the piano, I can't work on the computer. I'm stuck here in this chair forever, I can't get up! I can't get up." I clutched her arm in anguish. At that moment, I really was unable to move.

Though no doubt I alarmed her, she didn't show it. "Would you like to try reading, just a little?" she suggested quietly.

I shook my head vigorously, No.

"Do you want to take a walk?"

No! I can't get up. I am stuck here, trapped, incapacitated.

"How about a nice warm bath?"

For a moment the prospect interested me, but when I pictured myself lying in the water, staring at the shower head, it was no good. The burden of time was particularly hard for me there. "No," I said. "I get frightened in the bath."

At last she eased me to my feet and guided me to the living room couch, where I sat, head in hands, while she made me a cup of soup and brought me a tranquilizer to swallow. The pill soon made me sleepy. I lay down, head on the armrest, and for a few minutes escaped into a light, fitful sleep.

When I awakened, I called my good friend Roger, the psychiatrist and meditation teacher, and told him all that had happened.

"Sounds like you're having a pretty hard time," he said. He promised to come by the next day.

At the appointed hour the doorbell rang, and I came to the door myself, leaning on my cane. "You're walking," he exclaimed as soon as he saw me. "You look great!"

This was the first time he had seen me since the hospital. I think he expected me to still be bedridden. As for looking great, I knew I was rail-thin, my face taut with fear, especially after yesterday's crisis. Still, it was nice for him to say so. Compared to the last time he saw me, I'm sure I seemed much improved.

We all adjourned to the sun deck and sat around the deck table. Roger, always soft-spoken and polite, took care to ask after Amy and our son. For a few minutes I tried to join in the small talk, but soon I burst out, "Roger, I need your help. My brain's all messed up. Something's wrong with my sense of time. A minute seems to last forever. And my attention span is minimal. I can't read, I can't watch television, I can't meditate. It feels like I can't do anything! Most days I just stare into space, waiting for the day to end."

Now the medical professional, he listened closely, observing my tone of voice, my gestures and body language.

Chin in hand, he took his time answering. "Well," he said finally, "you're probably right about the brain. Our sense of time is a very complex function. I'm not surprised that it's gone a bit haywire."

"I didn't notice it so much in the hospital."

"Probably you were focused on the hospital routines. Now that you're back home, your day is less structured, and time weighs more heavily on you. Besides, concentration and attention are all very high-level brain functions. They would be the last to repair themselves in your healing."

I grimaced. "I feel like I'm going to go crazy from this."

He shook his head and gave me his most reassuring smile. "No, I don't think so. Things might get pretty unpleasant for a while, and you might have an outburst or two, but patience is the key. Easy for me to say. If I were in your place, I'd have a hard time too."

Patience! How many times had I heard that advice. But Roger was different. He was my friend, my spiritual companion.

"But what can I do in the meantime?"

"Now that's an interesting question. Let me think." He took his time, contemplating the swaying pine boughs above our heads as he considered. "Tell me," he said finally, "Is there something you enjoy doing? Something that gives you pleasure?"

"Pleasure?" I laughed bitterly. "I've forgotten what pleasure feels like."

"Are you sure? Think about it."

I reviewed my few daily activities. "Well, dozing on the couch, with my eyes half closed, is tolerable. I don't feel the weight of time so much then. But I have this routine. I have my exercises, and daily walks, and reading, and playing the piano. And I just can't keep to it. Time is like glue, gumming up the works whenever I try to do anything."

Roger laughed. "Pascal had a saying about doctors. He said, 'The purpose of the physician is to keep the patient entertained while nature provides the cure.' I think you may be trying too hard."

"That's my nature," I interjected.

"I know, but now may not be the time for that. If lying on the couch gives you pleasure, by all means do that. Do it for several hours a day if it helps you. The so-called yoga of pleasure can be a genuine spiritual practice."

"Really?" I said, my tone dubious.

"Really. I've practiced it myself from time to time," he concluded with a chuckle.

My body went slack with the sudden release of the tension that had been building up for days. Don't try so hard. Such simple advice, but for someone for whom each hour was like molasses, a revelation. Roger had given me the permission I needed to trust my instincts, and surrender to them.

Surrender: weeks ago I had learned its value in the intensive care ward, when I yielded my fear to the comfort and care of the nurses. Apparently I had already forgotten that lesson, and Roger's suggestion was a timely reminder.

Later that evening Amy and I took a walk at sunset along a path bordering an estuary of San Francisco Bay. Usually our daily walk in the neighborhood was a challenge for me, but this time I felt my inner demons subside long enough for me to enjoy the feeding egrets, the darkening pink of the sunset, the silhouette of the hills, and a sense of pleasure and ease I had nearly forgotten.

As we headed back toward the car, I suddenly put my arm around her waist and said, "Let's go out to dinner tonight. I'm in the mood for Japanese."

And so we did. At the restaurant, one of our old familiar haunts, I looked at her sitting across the table from me and for the moment felt myself again. I reached out and took her hand. "This is like old times, isn't it?"

I saw the tears glistening on her cheeks, and I began to cry too. How hard this must have been for her, all these weeks being my constant nursemaid, confessor, and companion. I was so lucky to have someone like her in my life.

Our meal came, and we consumed it slowly, with delight. "Everything's going to be all right," I whispered, and she nodded.

Yes, everything's going to be all right.

That was a Sunday. I had three more days to bask in the glow of my new "yoga of pleasure," to let myself lie on the couch as long as I wanted. Three more days before the roof fell in and catastrophe struck. As I write this I am reminded of the old joke: "Just because you're paranoid doesn't mean that people aren't really out to get you." Just because my catastrophic fears, my "three terrors," were exaggerated didn't mean that something terrible couldn't happen.

And that Thursday, something did.

EIGHT

LIGHTNING STRIKES TWICE

One day, while Lazarus was out on his balcony, his wife brought him a tray of tea and sweet cakes. As Lazarus turned to greet her, he suddenly fell senseless to the ground, exactly as he had that fateful morning long ago. As his wife cried out for help, Lazarus' eyes snapped open and widened in fear as he realized he was unable to move. "All my healing has been lost!" he cried in fear as litter bearers arrived to carry him to the house of healing. "I am going to die again!"

One of our comforts in the face of grave misfortune is the thought, Thank goodness something this terrible can never happen again. A movie called *Fearless* explores the ramifications of this attitude. Its protagonist is one of the few survivors of a plane crash, and as he returns to his ordinary life, he begins to take absurd risks, like standing on the ledge of a skyscraper, his arms spread wide, convinced that his amazing good fortune has made him invulnerable.

But real life does not play according to any such rules, and fate can be capricious and cruel. We may read in the newspaper of a mother losing her only child in a car accident, only to discover that elsewhere that same day her husband has died of a heart attack. Such things do happen, but as Diane worked hard to help me understand, none of us can live effectively if we dwell on such remote possibilities.

In the five weeks since I had come home from Kentfield, in spite of my problems I was definitely improving. My balance and coordination were better, my sleep had stabilized, my sensory fog was slowly lifting, and my friend Roger had proposed what seemed an excellent solution to my battle with time. Even the lack of sensation in various parts of my body seemed to be diminishing. And I consoled myself with two thoughts: first, like the character in *Fearless,* I had survived the worst that fate could throw at me, and second, Dr. Doherty had promised me an eventual full recovery. However shaky my confidence, however difficult it was to struggle through each day, these two facts were my touchstones. Lightning never strikes twice in the same place, I thought. I was banking on that.

It was almost time for my follow-up appointment with Dr. Doherty, and for me to realize the "healing vision" I had created with Diane for this moment—to be walking more smoothly, to see improvement in my sensory fog, and to be helping my business. I was making progress on all three fronts. My walking was indeed improving, with each visit to the supermarket the sensory fog was less disturbing, and with my short daily stints of computer programming I was slowly completing an important project that no one else in the business could do. I was looking forward to sharing this progress with Dr. Doherty.

Roger's visit had been on a Sunday. In ten days I would see Dr. Doherty, but that Thursday I also had an appointment with Dr. Castleman's nurse to discuss the possibility of a new drug. My new sleeping drugs made me drowsy and, I thought, a little low during the day. One doctor had suggested a particular drug, an antidepressant which I will call Energexol, to combat this daytime drowsiness.

The actual decision to try this drug was mine, though Dr. Castleman, through his nurse, had already concurred that it might prove useful. My visit to the nurse was simply to obtain drug samples and a prescription. At this point I was willing to try anything to feel better. In spite of the comfort I felt lying on the couch, I didn't want to spend all day doing it.

So with a box of sample pills and a prescription in hand, I went home hopeful that this new drug would improve my spirits. I swallowed the first pill that very afternoon, just before an appointment with Diane. As Amy drove me to Diane's office, I remarked that I already felt brighter and more optimistic. As soon as I sat down in Diane's office, I said: "I'm taking an antidepressant now, and already I feel better." But as the session progressed, the good feeling waned, and by the end of the session I was feeling uneasy and anxious.

On our way home Amy and I stopped to buy coffee, and it was then I first noticed a change: my right hand was growing numb as it gripped my cane. My feet felt odd too—tingly and burning—and I was having more trouble keeping my balance. Later that evening, during dinner, I noticed I was having difficulty holding my fork.

The next day brought another disturbing symptom: whenever I stood up, I felt as though I were going to faint. Several times I had to sit down again and put my head between my knees. Immediately I called Dr. Castleman's office and spoke to the nurse.

"Oh, that is just orthostatic hypotension," she explained. "It's a common side effect of Energexol. You should adjust to it in two or three days."

"So it's all right to continue taking it?"

"Sure."

So, after staring with some trepidation at the next Energexol pill in my hand, I put it in my mouth and swallowed it.

But the fainting spells got worse, and by evening I was feeling quite strange. The increased lack of sensation that had begun in my hands and feet had spread throughout my body, even to places that had never been numb before. That night Amy and I went out to dinner at a Chinese restaurant. As I looked around the dining hall, I had a disturbingly familiar sensation: the faces of the diners looked dreamlike, overly bright, their conversation annoyingly loud. The sensory fog that had taken so long to subside had suddenly returned.

I put a hand up to my cheek. "How do I look?" I asked Amy.

She examined my face carefully. "Your eyes are strange."

"Different than you've seen before?"

She nodded. What she saw was what I felt—quite strange.

I was starting to become alarmed. What was happening to me?

That night my sedatives didn't work, and I wasn't able to sleep at all. All night an incredible nervous energy coursed through my body, and periodically I felt waves of anxiety, as intense as any physical pain, rise and fall in my stomach. When I awoke, and rubbed my legs together in bed, I realized I now had little sensation below the knees.

"Something bad is happening," I said to Amy as soon as

she awoke. "Something's wrong. We have to call Dr. Castleman's office."

Since it was a Saturday, I was connected to Dr. Castleman's on-call physician, a Dr. Jacobsen. In a voice shaking with agitation and dismay, I tried to explain what had happened. "It's a catastrophe!" I said. "All the encephalitis symptoms that have been healing for the past three months have come back."

"I doubt that is so," he replied. "But I'd better take a look at you. Could you meet me at the emergency room in half an hour?"

That hateful place! But I felt it was important to go. At the onset of my disease, my promptness in getting to the emergency room had saved my life. This time I was taking no chances.

At the emergency room Dr. Jacobsen said that he was familiar with my case. "I was one of the doctors monitoring you in your coma," he said. He also mentioned that he was a student of Buddhism, and had actually attended a lecture I had recently given. When he said that, I was embarrassed that he had to see me now in such an agitated state. But he tried to cheer me up.

"You're incredibly lucky. With a brain stem infection, you could have been 'locked in,' totally paralyzed, with an intact mind but no ability to communicate in any way. That can happen with your type of encephalitis."

I already knew that, but at the moment I felt far from lucky.

I proceeded to recount to him the events of the past

forty-eight hours, my experience with the Energexol, and all that followed. After listening carefully, he proceeded with a neurological exam. Blood work, he said, had already been completed by the emergency room staff, showing him that there was no infection present.

During the exam he noted my coordination difficulties and lack of sensation, but that was to be expected, he said, and pronounced me in reasonably good shape considering the severity of my coma. But I was not reassured. Since he had never seen me before, I felt he did not really grasp how much worse my symptoms were than before the Energexol. I tried once again to impress this point on him.

"I understand," he replied, " but healing from this disease is like healing from a major stroke. It's a marathon; it takes at least a year. You can expect setbacks along the way."

Setbacks? Setbacks in the healing process I could understand, but wasn't this different? This was a drug-induced setback. Couldn't it be reversed?

"You're taking quite a cocktail of drugs already, too many in my opinion," was his answer. "Whatever reaction you're having to the Energexol, it should wear off soon."

How soon?

"No more than two weeks, I should think."

Two more weeks of this agony. That was not what I wanted to hear. What a disaster! After all my months of daily struggle and hard work. I writhed in discomfort on the hospital bed, my face a clear mask of disappointment.

He smiled reassuringly. "I'm sorry," he said. "I wish

there were more I could do. Give me a call if anything changes. Incidentally," he added, " I really enjoyed your Buddhist lecture. Good luck to you."

Dr. Jacobsen had tried hard to be helpful, but in the end I felt I was no better off than before, and with no real insight into what was happening to me. That night I was again sleepless, as the waves of anxiety in my belly increased in intensity and frequency. Two nights in a row with no sleep. My old fears about being forever sleepless rose up to haunt me. I felt that whatever malady had seized me was taking me into territory I could not handle.

So I left an emergency message for Dr. Jacobsen, who promptly returned the call. He too was concerned about my lack of sleep, and prescribed a powerful sedative to combat it. "One pill will give you four hours or so of sound sleep. Take one right away. Then when you wake up take another. You have to get some sleep." Amy went out immediately to get the prescription filled, while I waited, curled up on the bed, my heart pounding.

The pill did make me sleep away the afternoon, and allowed two hours of slumber that night. It was now Monday morning, time for my long-awaited appointment with Dr. Doherty. I had been looking forward to this visit for so long as a benchmark of improvement and triumph. Instead I would be able to report to her only this new mysterious crisis. Perhaps she would have some insight into what was happening to me. I didn't know; I couldn't think about it. As we descended the stairs to the car, I was so tired I could barely stand.

We arrived at Kentfield and were immediately ushered into Dr. Doherty's office, where she greeted us with a bright smile. But as soon as I sat down and began to pour out my tale of woe, her expression changed to one of concern.

"Energexol," she repeated, frowning. "It sounds like some kind of adverse drug reaction."

"But all my encephalitis symptoms are back!" No one, even Dr. Doherty, seemed to fully appreciate how frightening that was to me, nor had anyone yet offered an explanation that made sense.

"That is strange," she admitted. "But there's no way a mere drug could reverse your physiological healing."

Well, perhaps not, but why did it feel that way to me? "Is there anything that can be done?"

I had already asked Dr. Jacobsen the same question, and Dr. Doherty gave me essentially the same answer, although not before looking in her physician's manual to read up on the side effects of Energexol. "Anxiety, insomnia, parasthesia," she read from the list. "Parasthesia means numbness. The symptoms you're having are all listed as side effects of the drug. If so, they should clear up soon."

We spoke for nearly twenty minutes longer, but I must have been too anxious to pay much attention, for I remember little of what was said. I do know that Dr. Doherty had me walk toe-to-heel and perform a few other exercises, and was pleased with what she saw. "You should think about joining a gym," was her recommendation. "Start building your strength back."

In other circumstances, that would have seemed like a ringing endorsement of my progress. But as things stood, I wasn't even sure I could manage a car ride, much less a gym. As we drove home, I leaned my head against the window in despair. I felt abandoned, alone with this frightening new development, which no one seemed to fully understand.

The moment I awoke the next morning from two hours of fitful sleep, I knew immediately that something was drastically wrong. For one thing, I was unable to get out of bed. I could still move my limbs; I was not paralyzed. But I could barely feel them. And though I still had the ability, I seemed to have lost the will to move. I felt completely disconnected from my body. And as soon as I opened my mouth to call for Amy I heard a strange and sinister sound, like a parent at a Halloween party trying to imitate a ghost for a circle of terrified children.

"Amy," I intoned, in this scary new voice, as she sat by the side of the bed holding both my hands in hers. "Amy. Amy."

"What is it, darling?" Her face was filled with concern, but not yet with fear.

I shook my head, squeezing her hands in mine, and writhed in discomfort. How could I explain it? "I don't know," I attempted. "It's coming. It's coming."

"What?" she said, stroking my face, my hair. "What is it?"

It was the panic, the most powerful wave yet, welling up from deep inside my belly and flooding my whole body. For a fleeting moment I pictured the scene in the movie *Alien* where the alien creature incubating inside a man's stomach gnaws its way out from the inside as the man screams and blood spatters. An alien power in my stomach—that's how it felt to me.

"It's over," I kept repeating. "It's over, it's over." This terrible state I was in would last forever, I would never recover from it. Of this I was suddenly certain. This was the end. All my tedious healing from the encephalitis had been for naught. This was not really a thought, but something much deeper, as though an auto-destruct switch had been turned on deep inside my brain. Some other part of my mind was still rational enough to realize that these scary dramatics I was displaying were illogical and unnecessary, but that thought had no force, it was no match for what felt like an alien power now controlling my body.

"Maybe you need more sleep," Amy suggested. "You haven't slept much the last few days."

"Maybe," I replied doubtfully, as the latest wave of panic slowly subsided.

"Here," she said, offering me one of Dr. Jacobsen's sleeping pills, "why don't you take one of these."

I took the pill, dubious that it would have any effect, but when I awoke with a start, a couple of hours later, the sunlight was streaming in through the window and the clock registered ten o'clock. I was alone. "Amy!" I cried out. She was downstairs, but soon came running.

"It's the same," I said, in that quavering, ghostlike voice. "The same. I can't get up."

"How about some breakfast?" she asked, trying gamely to steer me toward my usual routine. "Some juice and toast?"

I shook my head. "No, nothing." In my mind a bizarre thought had suddenly appeared, like a sinister stranger. A person can live without food for weeks, I thought, but without liquid for only two or three days. Two or three days, and I could be done with this agony. In my entire life, I had never had such thoughts, never contemplated such things, but somehow in my current state of mind they seemed appropriate, even necessary. I was not ready to speak them, though—not yet.

"No," I repeated. I clutched her hand tighter and looked up into her face, hopeful that through her I could find a passage back to the ordinary world, but her face seemed so far away. I was losing her, I thought, losing my grip, losing the world.

I tried to say more, tried to explain, but what came out was barely coherent. My chance for healing was finished, I tried to say, my chance for recovery over. I would be stuck in this living hell forever. I knew it. My body and mind told me, loud and clear. No one could help me. No one would save me. Not this time. Against all odds, lightning had struck me down twice, and this time I would not get up.

Amy listened patiently, as she always did. Over these months she had learned to weather whatever storm or crisis I created, knowing that sooner or later it always passed. At least until now.

"Have you taken your tranquilizer?"

I nodded. I had already taken two pills, half my allowable daily maximum.

"How about some juice?" she tried, offering me the glass. "You need some liquid."

I shook my head, remembering my earlier conviction that the way out of my dilemma was to forgo food and drink, but my physical urge to survive was far stronger than those self-destructive thoughts. I was thirsty, and hungry. I nodded weakly and took a few sips.

A little toast and jam, some juice—how good it tasted. But I was terrified that at any moment another panic attack would come. They were increasing in strength, and seemed purely physical, unconnected to anything I was thinking. It was the Energexol; I was certain of that. This drug that had been touted to me as harmless had destroyed all of my healing, and my doctors' reassurances that its effects would subside presently—a conclusion that fitted logic and common sense—were helpless against the force of my opposite conclusion. I was stuck like a needle in a broken record, caught by hopelessness and despair.

Nevertheless I struggled to maintain some command of my fate. "You have to do something," I told Amy. "You must call Dr. Castleman's office. Tell them it's an emergency."

At Dr. Castleman's office, a nurse was always available to come to the phone, who if necessary had immediate access to Dr. Castleman himself. The nurse Amy contacted happened to be the same one who had dispensed the drug to me the previous Thursday. She was shocked to hear what had happened, and promised to notify Dr. Castleman immediately and call us back.

I also had enough presence of mind to realize that this situation was becoming totally untenable for Amy. I couldn't bear to have her out of my sight, even for a moment. Even when she went downstairs for a moment to the kitchen or bathroom, I was consumed with anxiety. "You have to get help," I said to her. "You can't do this by yourself. I'm in bad shape now. Call Yvonne," I pleaded. "Ask Yvonne to come."

At first Amy demurred, saying it wasn't necessary, but I insisted. Yvonne, our best friend, the one who had comforted Amy and Ivan the day the doctors thought I would die, would surely know what to do. As it happened, she was home when Amy called and said yes, of course she would come. She was only twenty minutes' drive away.

While we were still awaiting the return call from Dr. Castleman's office, I heard the doorbell ring, and presently Yvonne entered my bedroom, Amy just behind her, and pulled up a chair next to my bed. "Hi, Lew," she said cheerily, as though nothing were amiss. Seeing her was a great solace to me. Yvonne, a Buddhist teacher with long experience in spiritual matters and in aiding people who were dying, had been our friend and Buddhist fellow traveler for thirty years. Her calm, no-nonsense demeanor steadied me considerably.

Forgetting that Amy surely must have filled her in on the telephone, I started to explain the whole situation—

the Energexol, my sleeplessness, the panic attacks, my sudden sense of psychic paralysis, but as I listened to myself speak in my ghost-party voice, I realized I wasn't making much sense. Yvonne seemed nevertheless to take it all in stride. She was as clear-eyed, capable, and solid as always.

While I was speaking, the telephone rang, and it was Dr. Castleman's nurse. Amy spoke to her in the next room, and then returned to apprise us of the news. Dr. Castleman had been informed of my situation and had left a message for a psychiatrist with whom he often collaborated to call us as soon as he could. My heart sank as I realized that I would have to endure more waiting. Still, it seemed that this psychiatrist was my best hope, and I focused all my attention on the telephone, waiting for it to ring again.

After a while, Yvonne and Amy finally managed to get me out of bed and downstairs, though I needed their help to walk, since I had almost no sensation in my legs or feet. I spent the remainder of the afternoon on the downstairs couch, wrapped in a blanket, crying out, whenever the phone rang, "It's him!" But invariably it would be some- one else.

While I sat in a near stupor, absorbed in my own inner hell, Amy and Yvonne chatted, like any two friends who have not seen each other for a while. What else could they do? There was nothing more for any of us to do but wait. Yet I was acutely aware of the contrast between the ordinariness of their conversation and the terror of my inner world.

At one point I could no longer bear my interior world

alone and began a long, incoherent monologue, hoping that somehow if I could just explain it well enough matters might improve. "A person should be allowed to decide," I rambled. "Like the samurai. A matter of honor. It should be a matter of choice, when and where, how it should happen, why it should happen. A person's life is his own responsibility."

Writing about it now, I shudder to think what effect this must have had on Amy especially, but at this point I was conscious of little but my own rapidly contracting universe of fear.

"Do you understand? Do you understand what I'm trying to say?"

"Yes, Lew, I understand," Yvonne answered, for both of them.

I was so grateful for her response. She did not challenge or judge me, or tell me to shape up and stop all this nonsense, as I feared she might. Nor did she show any fear or alarm. She accepted my reality just as it was, giving me the space and support I needed to be who I was, and say what I said, not agreeing or disagreeing, just acknowledging. The Buddhist way.

The phone rang. Once again I cried, "It's him," but no, it was Diane returning Amy's urgent message. She and Amy spoke for a while, and then Amy handed the phone to me. To Diane, my therapist, I was finally able to say the word that I had been bobbing and weaving to avoid the whole day. "Suicide. Have you ever had any patients who have been suicidal?"

"Yes," she answered. "Yes, I have. But Lew, listen to me. You don't need to start down that road. Amy has explained it all to me. You're having a bad drug reaction. That's all. Keep telling yourself that. Amy tells me a psychiatrist is going to call soon. Just hold on and wait for his call. He'll be able to help you. Don't give up hope. It's way too soon for that. Believe me. I've been down this road with other people. It's way too soon to even begin those thoughts."

In reply I rambled on and on, trying to make the conversation last as long as possible, clinging to her presence and her voice as though to a life raft. But eventually the conversation had to come to an end, with her repeating her admonitions and my saying "Thank you" over and over.

Then more waiting. As time passed, it occurred to me that the likely resolution of this situation was for me to go to the hospital, to a psychiatric ward. I couldn't imagine putting Amy through another day like this, nor could Yvonne drop her life and move in with us. No, this endless day couldn't be repeated. I began to fantasize what it would be like in the hospital. Would it be hell? It would, I was convinced of that. But what of the details? Would I be strapped down to a bed? Drugged into a stupor? Would there be bars on the windows? These thoughts terrified me, but at the same time it was a relief to think that I could at last be somewhere safe, releasing Amy from this ordeal I was forcing her to endure.

Afternoon turned to early evening. Even though I was

wrapped in a blanket, wearing a heavy sweater, I was still shivering. When would the doctor call? He was my last hope. Call, call, when would he call?

At last the phone rang. I cried out.

Amy went to the kitchen and answered. Yes! It was the doctor. At last! The two of them talked for a long time while I strained to hear her side of the conversation, which were mostly neutral responses like "Yes" and "I think so." Then at last she called to me, and it was my moment to speak to this man, this savior in my imagination, whose name I understood to be Dr. David James.

"Dr. James!" I shouted into the phone. And all in a rush my story poured out, the Energexol, the waves of panic, the sleeplessness, the return of my encephalitis symptoms, the numbness, the fog, and finally, my thoughts of self-destruction. In the midst of my monologue I was careful to include the fact that I was a successful businessman, author, and musician—I suppose to impress this doctor that I was not some ordinary hysteric but a person of consequence. As he began to respond and ask questions, I was immediately struck by his calm, deliberative manner. However loudly the alarm bells were going off in my head, there were none I could detect in his. I also detected a pronounced Bostonian accent. Taking notice of his flat *a*'s was a momentary distraction that I found strangely comforting.

"How can Energexol do this to me?" I asked, and Amy gestured to me to lower my voice. I realized I had been shouting. "How can it make the encephalitis come back?"

"I don't know," he said. "I don't have enough information at this point. We need to examine you and do some testing. You're starting to have some pretty unpleasant thoughts, too, so we need to deal with that right away. That means trying various drugs to see which one is best for you."

"You mean at the hospital?" The gates of hell were looming.

He was careful in his response. "Well, at the hospital, the whole process would go a lot faster. Ordinarily you would go into a neurological unit, but we don't have one here, so I'd have to admit you to the psychiatric unit. That's the only place you'd have the kind of constant observation we need. It won't be pleasant, but you shouldn't need to be there more than a few days. Do you want to do that?"

I was in no condition to make any decisions. Why didn't he just tell me what to do? I thought again of Amy, and of this terrible day. "I don't think I can put my wife through another day of this," I told him. But at the same time, all my worst fantasies of a psychiatric ward began swirling through my brain.

Dr. James then started to outline the practical steps involved in admitting me to the hospital that very evening, but I was too distraught to follow the details, and suggested he work it all out with Amy. His last words before I handed the phone back to her were, "I'll be in to see you at the hospital tomorrow as soon as I can."

Tomorrow. I couldn't begin to imagine a tomorrow. But

he would be coming to see me. He would be there to help me. That was something, however slender, to hang my hat on.

We drove to the hospital in Yvonne's Volvo station wagon, Amy in the front and I in back, wrapped in a blanket. This was the same drive, lost to memory, that I had made three months ago, in nausea and delirium, to the emergency room. What was going to happen? What was in store for me? I didn't know. I couldn't think about it. All I could think of was holding myself together, as the car headlights and other illuminations of the night flashed by in a blur.

The admissions process at the emergency room seemed interminable. Over in one corner, Amy was taking care of all the paperwork while I sat hunched over in the waiting area with Yvonne. I was glad she was comfortable sitting in silence, because after all that had happened, I had nothing left to say. At long last I was put into a wheelchair and ushered into an examining room, where first a physician, and then a social worker, examined and questioned me. Dr. James had prepared the way by calling ahead, making sure that there was a bed for me, and explaining my situation, but I still had to repeat to the hospital personnel the circumstances that had brought me here. And when the social worker asked, "Are you having thoughts of suicide?" I stopped for a moment.

Yes, earlier in the day those thoughts had marched through my brain, but since talking to Dr. James and feeling that help was on the way, the impulses had subsided. I knew from my earlier experiences with the mental health system, when I was a Buddhist priest and sometimes brought people in crisis to the hospital, that in order for my admission to the psychiatric unit to be assured, I had to demonstrate danger of harm to myself or others. So I answered as I thought I needed to, "Yes."

"And do you have a plan?" the social worker continued.

A plan? What did she mean? Of course I didn't have a plan. It was all just talk, wasn't it? Suddenly I was ashamed that my panicky ramblings of earlier in the day had come to this. How could I have possibly sunk so low so fast? Then I remembered something I had once read: even for experts, it is impossible to tell when someone's thought of suicide is just talk, and when it is serious. I realized that the social worker's question was not a judgment or criticism of me personally. She was just trying to do her job.

"No, no," I protested shaking my head. "No plan."

At last the interview was over, I was deposited into a wheelchair once again and taken up an elevator, Amy at my side. There we were buzzed through the locked door of Unit A, the psychiatric unit, and ushered inside. In contrast to the rest of the hospital, which was brightly lit, this place was shadowy and dark, except for the lamps by the nursing station. A male nurse greeted me—apparently I was expected—introduced himself as Ralph, wheeled me over to a nearby table, sat down with a clipboard in front of him, and picked up a ballpoint pen.

Now there were more questions, more forms to fill out,

more administrative processing. Chin in hand, eyes fixed on the tabletop before me, I made my perfunctory responses. Every so often I would furtively glance about, trying to get my bearings in these spooky new surroundings.

"Will I have my own room?" I asked at one point.

"Yes," Ralph, answered. "You'll have a private room for now."

That was a relief. I didn't know if I could face the prospect of sharing a room with other people at this point.

At last it was over and I was shown to my room, a tiny cubbyhole just large enough for a bed, a chair, and a tiny bathroom. I noticed, as I washed my hands and dried them, that there was no towel rack, no place to hang the linen. I had had to leave my belt and the sash of my bathrobe at the nurse's desk, and it took me a while to understand why. Now it dawned on me that the absence of the towel rack was for the same reason: to prevent the patient from harming himself. If I had any doubts, now I knew for sure that in entering this place I had left the ordinary world far behind.

It was now after midnight. Soon Amy would have to leave, and I would be alone in this sinister place. I clung to her, trying to stretch the time out as long as possible. Visiting hours were strict here; I would not be able to see her again until six o'clock the following evening. But Dr. James would be coming. He had said so. Tomorrow something would happen.

I gulped the powerful sedative that Ralph brought to my room to help me sleep, and climbed into bed.

"Good night," I said to Amy. "Good-bye. I love you." Tears of exhaustion and despair welled up. "I love you so much."

She kissed me on the forehead. "I love you too." Then with a final hug, she turned away, closed the door behind her, and was gone.

I didn't go to sleep immediately but crouched on my knees on the bed, my head in the pillow, quietly moaning, over and over again, "Please help me, please help me."

There were nurses circulating through the halls, checking on the patients. I could hear them. But my voice was muffled by the pillow. Besides, this was a psychiatric unit. In this environment, such behavior would not cause alarm.

In any case, no one came. No one responded.

I was alone.

Lightning can and does sometimes strike twice. As I look back on the events of this awful day, I realize how much I had relied on Dr. Doherty's encouraging words—"You'll probably recover one hundred percent, most of your healing should be done by December"—as gospel truth, a prediction written in stone. The evidence of my slow, steady improvement in the weeks I was home from Kentfield also buoyed me. Every day, regardless of my mood, I could say to myself, over and over, "I *am* getting better."

But as irritating as I found Dr. Jacobsen's remark that in this long marathon of healing I should expect some setbacks, he was right. No one could have predicted the effect the Energexol would have on my healing brain. Much later, Dr. James would say to me, "If it had been me, I probably would have prescribed it for you too."

The events of this "black Tuesday" were a chance intersection of the particulars of my disease, the stage of my healing, the neurological impact of the drug, and my own psyche and personality.

Now in the face of this new catastrophe, once again I had to confront the fundamental insight of the Buddha—everything changes, nothing lasts—without the psychological defenses of a healthy person. It was like hearing an old, familiar spiritual lesson shouted at me through a giant megaphone. We live in a world where lightning does strike, all the time, everywhere. Some days our luck is good; on others it is bad, very bad.

My biggest mistake on this day of dread was forgetting that the Buddha's lesson on impermanence applies to misfortune too. My conviction that my sorry state would last forever was an understandable but costly error. I should have remembered that everything changes. *Everything,* even hell on earth. But it would be a while yet before I had the presence of mind to recapture that insight. Until then, sequestered in my tiny hospital room, I was indeed alone.

NINE

DESPAIR

Lazarus lay in the house of healing, silent and unmoving, his eyes staring fixedly at the ceiling, as his physicians tried various remedies. His pulses were strong; he had no fever, or other obvious signs of serious illness. But to all attempts to communicate he was mute and unresponsive. "What ails him?" one of the physicians muttered to the Master Healer. "He was doing so well. What strange affliction could suddenly bring him this low?"

The Master Healer took his time before answering, and when he did, his voice was a mere whisper. "Despair," he finally replied. "Despair."

Over the gate of Hell in Dante's Inferno are emblazoned the words "Abandon hope, all ye who enter here." I had been familiar with this famous stanza all my life, but never until now did I comprehend the full terror its words implied. All of us, whatever our circumstances in life, must harbor some hope within our hearts, or we cannot continue. Like anyone, I have had my share of life difficulties, but not once, even during my years-long struggle with cancer, did I ever lose hope.

I know well, however, that some people are constitutionally afflicted with deep despair. I had met many of them when I was active as a Buddhist priest; I had counseled them, sat up all night with them, driven them to the local hospital, in fact to the same ward where I was now housed. I remember one young woman who, after struggling for years with hallucinatory voices, eventually ended her suffering by jumping off the Golden Gate Bridge. I helped conduct her funeral.

This chapter, which tells of my own experience of despair, has not been easy to write. But I hope that it manages to convey two important truths. First, if such a thing could happen to me—cheery and upbeat by nature—then it could happen to anyone. And second, people who have lived with hopelessness for months or years are deserving of our deepest compassion. The Buddha himself died in great physical pain though his mind was calm, and he taught repeatedly that mental suffering, not physical suffering, is the true human dilemma. In our society, those who suffer mentally must endure against formidable odds. Their plight is indeed difficult.

So if you keep these two points in mind as you read this portion of my tale, you will have redeemed my purpose in writing it.

I awakened in my tiny room while it was still dark. By the glow of my wristwatch I saw it was 5:15 A.M. For a moment I was disoriented. Where was I? Then the events of the previous day came flooding back. I was a patient in Unit A, a psychiatric ward, alone in gloom, with no idea what was to come next. Earlier in the night, when my first sleeping pill had worn off, I had wrapped myself in my sashless bathrobe and stumbled across the darkened day room to ask at the nursing station for another pill. The night nurse did not seem too friendly. "One pill should be enough," she remarked.

"I'm allowed another one if I need it," I explained plaintively. Dr. James had assured me that my current regimen of pills would be retained. "I had viral encephalitis," I added, hoping that bit of explanation would help.

"You had that in July," she responded sternly, now consulting my chart. "This is October." She seemed to think I didn't know what month it was. But perhaps she didn't realize that viral encephalitis takes so many months of healing. Soon Dr. James would fill my chart full of explanations and instructions, and the staff would then understand that I was not a usual psychiatric patient. But as yet she only knew the sketchy facts recorded in my chart when I was admitted. My chart must have mentioned the extra sleeping pill, for she did finally give it to me, and I was able to sleep for a few more hours.

After waking, I lay in bed for more than an hour, listening for sounds of life, but there were none. Apparently the denizens of this place kept later hours than I did. I got out of bed and fumbled with my clothes, dressing as best as I could though my hands, legs, and much of my body were numb. Then, picking up my cane, I hobbled out into the hallway to explore my new surroundings.

The unit was a simple quadrangle of rooms surrounding a large central day room, furnished with couches, chairs, dining tables, a Ping-Pong table, and a spinet piano. At this hour the central space was all dark, illuminated only by the lights of the nursing station in the corner. A snack kitchen occupied one whole wall. As I made my first circuit of the hallways, I noticed that directly across from the nursing station were two small rooms. Through the open door of one I could see a tiny enclosure, empty but for a plain mat on the floor. The second one was locked shut, but through its tiny window a wide-eyed young man stared out, knocking slowly and steadily against the pane of wire-reinforced glass, mouthing inaudible words. A chill coursed down my spine. Would this be my fate too, if I could not contain myself?

I quickly returned to my room and hid under the bed-clothes.

At about 8:00 A.M. a nurse poked her head in my door-way to tell me it was breakfast time. She then added that Dr. James had called and would be coming soon. My heart skipped a beat. All my thoughts were focused on the moment I would meet this man who was to help me.

I emerged to find about fifteen other patients already seated at the dining tables with their trays of food. "Richmond," one of the staff called out. I raised my hand. When he saw my cane, he brought my tray to my place at the table. I thanked him, taking a bit of comfort in the knowledge that I already had a place here, already a tray with my name on it. I looked down at the food—liberal portions of everything, scrambled eggs, toast, bacon, juice—and for a moment fantasized once again that if I didn't eat or drink, my torment would soon end, but my hunger was far stronger than my fantasy. I found myself welcoming the distraction of food, and quickly wolfed down everything on the plate.

Meanwhile, I eyed the others with curiosity and ner-vousness. They were a diverse lot, some young, some old, some well dressed, some still in disheveled nightclothes, but they were mostly unremarkable, except for the fact that they ate in near total silence—no conversation, no idle chatter, no interaction. Everyone—including me, I suppose—was lost in his or her own private world.

The awful panic that had brought me here was already rising in my craw, just as a staff member brought me a tiny paper cup containing two pills, and a glass of water. "Your morning meds," he said. I recognized them as the tranquilizer I had already been taking for weeks, and I quickly gulped them down. But they seemed to do little good. After half an hour, I was distraught as ever. When would Dr. James come?

My plan was to wait quietly on my bed for his arrival, but a disturbing new symptom prevented that. After a few minutes in bed, I could not sit still. I had an irresistible craving to move, to leap up and stump with my cane up and down the halls until I was exhausted. Then I would rest, but only until the urge to pace overcame my fatigue, and I leaped up again.

The rest of the day was a blur. As I limped around and around the compound, all my attention was focused on the clock. Once a nurse approached me to tell me that Dr. James had called again. He had been delayed, but wanted to assure me that he was still coming. It was considerate of him to keep me informed, but it was also terribly hard to keep waiting. Other than that brief contact, and the momentary diversion of lunch, I was left to my own devices.

I had already spoken to Amy from the one pay phone available to patients, and told her about my new disturbing symptom, this constant pacing.

"Just try to hold on," she said, "and wait for Dr. James. Remember, I'll be there at six."

But at four o'clock Dr. James still hadn't come, and I had collapsed on my bed for good, worn out from my exertions. I was beginning to give up hope when my door swung open and a tall, kindly-looking man in his late fifties entered, moving with the controlled grace of an athlete, and took his seat next to me.

"Hello," he said, extending his hand. "I'm Dr. James."

I sat up in bed with some difficulty and shook his hand while I studied his face. It was as serene as the voice I remembered on the telephone, with good-humored crinkles around his eyes and a reassuring smile. Once again I was struck with the contrast between his calm deliberateness and my anxiety.

"How are you feeling?" he asked with studied casualness.

All the pent-up frustration of the day came pouring out in a frenzied description of all that had happened and a catalog of all my symptoms, new and old—the numbness, the unbearable anxiety, the return of my sensory fog, and this sudden new compulsion to pace.

"It feels like there's a firecracker in my head," I said at one point, hoping that Dr. James would know what I meant, that this catastrophic mental collapse would make some sense to him.

But he just listened patiently, head in hand, until I was done.

"How could taking one pill make all my encephalitis symptoms come back?" was my final question.

"Well, that's the question we have to explore," Dr. James replied. "Dr. Castleman and I have already discussed this at length. We're not sure yet what has happened to you, and the encephalitis is certainly a factor, but we don't think it is directly to blame."

"But all my healing has been destroyed! All the symptoms I started with—the numbness, the brightness, the loud sounds—they're all just as bad as when I began. And now I have this terrible anxiety and restlessness! Even right after the coma, it was never like this. And I can't do anything. I can't read, I can't watch television, I can't write. I can barely think."

Since the pacing was a new symptom, Dr. James asked me to describe it in detail. Was there any particular time of day it seemed better or worse? Did my doses of tranquilizer medication have any effect? I tried to answer his questions as best I could, but in truth I hadn't been keeping track. The whole day had been an agonizing blur.

"What kind of drug is Energexol?" I asked. "Are these typical side effects?"

"No, they're not. Energexol is a common antidepressant, and it generally helps people feel better. But your encephalitis apparently was a complicating factor—just how, we don't know yet."

"What can be done about it?"

"Well, first I need to increase the amount of tranquilizer you're receiving so you're less agitated. Then we'll start experimenting with drugs that might reverse your symptoms. The first one Dr. Castleman and I want to try is a drug called Neurontin."

Another strange drug! Given what one drug had done to me, I was fearful of taking any other. "What is it?"

"It helps normalize nerve communication. Often that can address the kinds of symptoms you're having."

"But not always?"

Dr. James could only offer me his kindly smile. "If it doesn't work, then we'll try something else. There are many options. That's one of the reasons you're here, so you can be under constant observation while we try these drugs. Here we can do in a matter of days what it might take weeks to do at home." He paused. "I also want you to take some psychological tests. That will help me understand better what is going on in your brain."

"What kind of tests?" Even at Kentfield, I had been fearful of tests and what damage to my mental functions they might reveal.

"Don't worry," he reassured. "I'll have Dr. Claussen come over from Berkeley to do the tests. She works with me all the time, and she's a wonderful person. I'm sure you'll like her."

I liked Dr. James. However strangely I spoke or behaved, he remained calm—a demeanor that was itself a powerful medicine. It might have been a professional facade, but I would soon realize that it was not, it was just who he was. If he was worried about me (and he confided to me many months later that in these first few days he was), he didn't show it. What he displayed to me instead was a rock-solid confidence, and the fact that he already had a well-thought-out plan for me.

"You're going to get better," he said as he stood up to leave. "If someone asked me in court to swear to that on a Bible, I would say yes."

That certainly gave me a sorely needed jolt of encouragement, though I didn't really believe it.

"And remember," were his parting words at the door, "whatever happens, I won't ever give up on you."

Those final words were a true blessing. After meeting me for fifteen minutes, already he was ready to give me that kind of commitment. I lay back in bed, closed my eyes, and heaved a shaky sigh of relief. I was no longer alone. Dr. James was with me.

It was now almost six o'clock, time for Amy's first visit. At about five-thirty I positioned myself across the day room in a spot where I could see the outside door and watched it constantly until I finally saw her familiar face through the glass and heard her being buzzed in. After a quick embrace in the hall we went straight to my room, where I collapsed on the bed in a heap of tears. She sat on the bed next to me, stroking and soothing me, as I told her all about my meeting with Dr. James, the drugs he wanted to try, the tests that were to come, the fact that my life and whole future—which had come to a dead stop the previous day—had been nudged ever so slightly into motion again.

Beyond that, there wasn't much for me to say. It was enough for her to be there, for the outside world to be made tangible again by her presence. While she stroked my hair and rubbed my back, I took pleasure in that most elemental of human gestures, the kindness of touch. She had brought some personal articles we had forgotten in the previous night's rush—my toothbrush, my beard trimmer and shaver (which, being sharp, had to be kept in the nurses' station), some more underwear and shirts. She stayed with me that night as long as the hospital rules allowed. Toward the end I was so sedated that she just sat close to me, reading a book, while I dozed, until the time came for my sleeping pill and lights out.

That next day I phoned her first thing in the morning. "I feel better this morning," I said. "Not good, but better."

"Yes, I can hear it in your voice," she responded. It was encouraging to hear her say that.

But two hours later I reached her again, this time on her cell phone. "It's all going south," I moaned, now feeling the "firecracker" exploding in my brain and the urgent compulsion to pace.

That's how the next day went, up and down. On the much higher dose of tranquilizing medication Dr. James had now prescribed for me, at times I felt reasonably in control of myself, but at others I was afraid I was losing my mind.

In my more lucid periods, I made an effort to introduce myself to each of the staff, explaining to them the special nature of my condition, that I had had a near-fatal case of viral encephalitis and now was suffering a kind of chemically enhanced post-traumatic stress. In spite of my experience during my first night, and my stereotypes of psychiatric hospital staff, I found them to be most patient and kind, not just to me but to all the patients. Whether it was because of their training or their long familiarity with mental patients, they rarely became irritable or raised their voices.

One patient, a young woman who had arrived in an acute manic state, demanded constant attention, and would run across the room from one staff member to another, demanding answers to questions like, "How do you spell 'boy'?" And the staffer, already busy with multiple responsibilities, would always take the time to reply, "B-O-Y, Betty, B-O-Y." He acknowledged her reality, however bizarre.

I also noticed that part of the daily schedule included a period of Buddhist mindfulness meditation, led by a staff member who had studied with one of my Buddhist colleagues. What a small world, I thought, and what an irony. How quickly our station in life can change, how suddenly fate can twist our life in uncanny knots.

The next afternoon the door to my room opened, and an attractive woman of middle age entered and introduced herself as Dr. Claussen, the neuropsychologist colleague of Dr. James. She deposited an oversize handbag on the floor and took her seat with a casual now-where's-my-pencil air that I suspected was a tactic to put patients at ease.

As she extracted notebooks and folders from her bag in preparation for the tests, she offered a steady stream of reassuring comments. "Now dear, I hear you've been thinking of doing something dumb. Now you mustn't think those things, because before long you're going to be fine and all this will be behind you."

By "something dumb," I assumed that she was referring to my suicidal thoughts, and that Dr. James had already briefed her in detail on my history and condition.

"You think so?" I answered. I was not obsessed with those self-destructive thoughts at the moment, but as I looked back on the time when I was, they seemed appropriate to my desperate situation. But Dr. Claussen seemed determined to disavail me of any such notions.

"Absolutely!" she announced, as she stacked various printed materials on the tiny table next to her chair. "I had a concussion once, when I was in graduate school. The boom of a sailboat smacked me in the head. It took me a year to recover. But I did. And look at me now." And she sat down next to me on the bed.

Then the tests began. The first one was a Rorschach, or inkblot, test. I was certainly familiar with the concept of such a test, but I had never taken one and was dubious that it would reveal anything of value. But I dutifully tried to provide some sort of interpretation for each of the pictures she showed me. She wrote down everything I said, word for word, sometimes asking me to repeat myself so she could record the exact expression I had used.

Then it came time for the MMPI, the Minnesota Multiphasic Personality Inventory. She handed it to me, a blur of small-printed questions with boxes, and I recoiled. "No," I protested, retreating to the room's other chair and beginning to rock back and forth in agitation. "I can't read, I can't think. You'll have to ask me the questions."

"All right, then," she said, and read me the list of questions for as long as I had the attention span to answer them. "Do I have fears about my health?" YES! "Do I sometimes think I am losing my mind?" YES! The questions went on and on.

The last test was an intelligence diagnostic. I was especially leery of this one, frightened what it would reveal about my mental capacities.

"What is the capital of Italy?"

"Rome."

"Recite the number 7423143 backward."

"3413247."

"As gentle is to anger, rough is to . . . ?"

Tricky. What was the opposite of anger? "Kindness." I was growing impatient and afraid. "How bad is it? How much have I lost?"

"Shush, dear, you're scoring high on every question. Let's just finish the test."

Then she was gone, and I was left to my own devices, to watch the clock, wander the halls, pace to exhaustion, and wait until the climax of the day, 6:00 P.M., when Amy would come.

From time to time I was able to shift my attention away from myself long enough to observe my fellow patients. I had expected more bizarre behavior and obvious manifestations of mental illness, but in most cases, except for a withdrawn, preoccupied air, their outward behavior was not that unusual. Gradually, as I overheard snippets of conversation between themselves and the staff, social workers, or doctors, I began to understand that though their illness itself, though controlled by medication, was suffering enough, what was worse was the simple effort of living in a world unsympathetic to their needs. One woman was afraid that if her boss were to discover that she was not just out sick but confined to a psychiatric ward, he would fire her. Another woman, addicted to pills and alcohol and severely depressed, wanted desperately to stop smoking. When one of the other patients scoffed, "Oh, Nicorette. It never works. I've tried it," the woman burst into tears. Stopping smoking, a difficult enough challenge even for a healthy person, was something in her anguished life she needed and wanted to master.

Once at lunch I sat across from a slender, bearded man who had once, he said, been a high-ranking government official. After a few halting efforts at conversation, his story began to come out. Some thirty years ago, he said, he had been stationed abroad in the middle of a violent civil war. Each morning he had to traverse the hundred yards between his apartment building and his office with a submachine gun in hand, crouching behind parked cars to protect himself from snipers.

One day he returned from work to find that the apartment where he and his family lived had taken a direct mortar hit, and the bodies of his wife and young son lay crumpled in the ashes. Later he buried their wedding rings in Italy, his ancestral country, and in the decades since had been unable to overcome his grief and despair. I expressed my condolences as best I could.

"Oh, you think that's bad," he said, forcing a smile. "What's really bad is that this damn place can't even find me a bed to sleep in tonight. I can't stay here—no insurance—and there's not a single bed in a single shelter in the whole county. I've been talking to the social workers all day, and they can't do a damn thing for me."

His comment confirmed what I had slowly been realizing—that this unit, plush and well run as it was, was not really a place of long-term treatment or healing, just a temporary way station. I heard one of the staff comment that the average patient stay was ten days. And this was in one of the most affluent counties in the nation. Now I understood the phrase "mental health care crisis" from an insider's perspective. These people were only here because of some life-threatening crisis in an otherwise long-term, chronic struggle with debilitating illness.

Two days after Dr. Claussen's visit, Dr. James spent all of his time with me explaining the results of her tests, especially the Rorschach. I had always thought of the Rorschach as highly subjective, but Dr. James produced a sheaf of papers full of graphs, numbers, and statistical scores, explaining that in the nearly hundred years since its invention, the Rorschach test had become more scientific, with elaborate computer programs to help interpret it.

His explanations were detailed and thorough, and I appreciated his implicit assumption that I had the capacity to follow the complexity of his presentation. But I was so absorbed in my own physical sensations that it was difficult for me to pay close attention. I did take notice, however, when he said "resource number" was very high.

"What's resource number?"

That score, he explained, describes how well a person

can endure a difficult ordeal, such as being held hostage. Five was considered a high score; mine was twelve.

That was impressive on paper, I thought, but right now I felt anything but resourceful.

"Is there a score for crazy?" I asked.

"As a matter of fact there is," he said, riffling through the papers. "And yours is zero." He looked up. "And there's a score for logic, too, and yours is exceptional. Most people ordinarily make a few logical mistakes when they interpret the images, such as seeing a "pink bear," but you didn't make any. You could get a job as a logician."

I didn't respond. My mind felt as though it were full of wet cement, and regardless of what the test said, at this moment I felt devoid of any logical skills.

"Now, hypervigilance," he said, turning to another page and showing me a graph that appeared to go off the top of its chart. "Hypervigilance occurs when a person is overly concerned with their own internal and external well-being, and yours, as you can see, is extremely high."

Of course it was high. I didn't need a test to tell me that.

When Dr. James began to explain how hypervigilance is a defense mechanism developed in response to a child-hood trauma, I became annoyed. Was this going to be some psychoanalytic pretext to dismiss my symptoms as overblown hysteria? What about the Energexol? I had the same childhood history before I took it as after. Yes, I had my share of childhood traumas, including my mother's death when I was four—but what did it matter now?

It mattered, Dr. James patiently continued, not because it was the sole cause of my panic but because it was a contributing factor over which I could exercise some control. Try to distract yourself from too much obsession with your own condition, he said. Try attending some of the group events that were part of the daily schedule.

I told him I had tried, but even to sit still for a five-minute staff-patient meeting was too much for me.

"There's method to my madness," he countered. "Involvement in activities will help you compartmentalize your anxiety and take your mind off it. Just make the effort. That's all I ask."

The next day I gave it a try, and crept down the hall to the door of the arts and crafts room. I peered in and saw that it was already filled with other patients doing what seemed to me quite complex tasks with paintbrushes, glass mosaic, and puzzle pieces. The room itself was full of a bewildering array of arts and crafts equipment stacked on shelves and counters. Hesitantly I took a chair, feeling like a kindergartner on his first day of school.

A staff member recognized me and came over right away. "What would you like to do, Lewis?" she said.

I shook my head. I was overwhelmed by the cacophony of voices and the confusion of colors and shapes around me. I had no idea how to answer her question. Suddenly I spotted a blue crayon in the center of the table. "Color," I muttered. "Maybe I could color with crayons."

She supplied me with a coloring book and box of crayons, and for about fifteen miserable minutes I tried to color a line drawing of a peacock. This is what I have been reduced to, I thought as I scribbled on the paper, a five-year-old child. Every minute I stayed I became more depressed, as the compulsion to leap up and resume pacing in the hall grew and grew. Finally, with a mumbled excuse, I got up and left, feeling as I did so that I had failed myself and Dr. James in this simplest of tasks.

Much later, when I described this frightening event to him, Dr. James explained that this sense of not being able to perform simple tasks is called psychiatric "impotence," and can be caused both by organic brain dysfunction and anxiety.

That night, when Amy came for her daily visit, I was still depressed about this incident. All the other patients seemed to be able to perform ordinary tasks with ease—read a newspaper, watch television—but because of my agitation, mental confusion, and sensory overload, I couldn't do any of these things. I had tried, but my attention span, so irritatingly brief even when I was home, now seemed nonexistent.

"I'm in the worst shape of anyone here," I muttered to Amy as she was rubbing my back.

She drew back sharply. For one of the few times since the onset of my illness, she appeared angry with me. "How can you say that?" she retorted. "That's not at all true! How can you give up so easily?"

Her perception, and Dr. James's too, was that each day I was improving a bit, less distraught and confused. But I had no sense of that. And now I had just told her that I was worse off than a ward full of chronic depressives and psychotics. No wonder she was angry. I began apologizing profusely, as I realized how self-pitying my comment must have sounded. After a few minutes we both calmed down, and she resumed her back massage. But I noticed an interesting shift in my mood. Her anger, far from discouraging me, had actually mobilized me. Suddenly I felt a bit stronger, a bit more willing to keep fighting, keep struggling. I suppose I had been so lost in my own suffering that her anger was a welcome jolt.

Some days were better than others. The following Sunday was a good day. I was calm and collected enough to play some pocket billiards. I joined a group discussion outside in the garden for about twenty minutes. Later I played one of my piano compositions on the out-of-tune spinet piano, eliciting enthusiastic applause from patients and staff alike.

Late that afternoon Dr. James and Dr. Castleman visited me together. The two of them sat in the garden while Amy and I sat side by side facing them on a wooden bench. The staff had briefed the two doctors on my successes of the day, and the doctors were encouraged, both by what they had heard from the staff and by my demeanor, which was considerably calmer and more lucid than they had previously seen.

"If this trend continues," Dr. James remarked, "you should be able to go home soon." Dr. Castleman nodded his concurrence. In their minds, these improvements were a sign that the Neurontin was finally taking effect.

But by the next day my perceived improvements seemed to have vanished, and I was once again calling Amy every two hours on her cell phone to tell her that things were "going south." Later that day I related this new discouragement to Dr. James, who in turn reported to me that the manufacturer of Energexol had finally responded to his inquiries to say that they had no record of a drug reaction similar to mine. My case was apparently one of a kind, another discouragement. But I suppose I should not have been surprised. How often had Energexol been given to someone five months into healing from a near-fatal case of viral encephalitis, itself a rare disease?

Meanwhile, I had new troubles to report to Dr. James. As my dosage of Neurotin had slowly increased, I was starting to experience strange new symptoms.

"I'm having difficulty swallowing," I told Dr. James. "Particularly at night, after dinner. Sometimes it takes me a minute or two just to swallow a sip of water. And sometimes my speech is slurred. Could that be a side effect of Neurontin?" I omitted to mention the worst-case scenario that my panicky mind had already conjured up to accompany this symptom. If I couldn't swallow, I wouldn't be able to eat or drink. I would be intubated again, bedridden, imprisoned. I would become a vegetable.

"I don't know," he said. "Possibly." He paused and cocked his head. "Now that you mention it, I can hear the change in your speech."

That evening, Amy and I debated for what seemed the hundredth time what to tell our friends and associates about my condition. She wanted to tell the truth, but would defer to my feelings. And I quickly realized that in spite of all my years helping the mentally ill in my role as a Buddhist priest, I was ashamed to let anyone know I was in a psychiatric unit. I thought I had a more enlightened attitude about mental illness than most, but apparently not when it came to my own situation.

This time we finally decided on what was in essence a cover story—that I was back in the hospital due to a bad drug reaction (that much was certainly true) and, being sedated, could talk to no one. This version of events would suffice for a few days, perhaps a couple of weeks, but what then?

I didn't even want Ivan, my grown son, to see me in my present condition, but out of concern for me he had telephoned Dr. James, and the two of them had a long, frank conversation about my situation.

"Your son is a very intelligent, perceptive, young man," Dr. James told me after that conversation. "He's very concerned about you."

"I know," I said. "But I don't want him to see me like this."

Thus far Dr. James had been gentle and tolerant of my irrational fears and fantasies, but this time he had a strong point of view and did not hesitate to express it. "On a scale of one to ten, I would say having your son visit you is a twelve. You should see him. Soon."

That admonition, like Amy's flash of anger, brought me up short. So the next evening when Amy came to visit, Ivan accompanied her. I was most apprehensive about my ability to hold myself together in his presence, but Ivan quickly reassured me that all that mattered to him was that he could see me, which he was clearly so happy to do. The sedatives I was taking had been building up all day, so I was lying in bed in a drugged stupor, and all I could do was lift my hand to take his.

"Thanks for coming, Ivan," I said, my speech a bit slurred from the drugs. "It's so good to see you." Tears wet my eyes. "Your Dad's in pretty bad shape," I added.

"It's okay, Dad, it's okay."

I realized, as I lay there, Ivan and Amy seated next to me, all holding hands, that for one of the few times since the onset of my illness we were together once again, our little family. And all the twenty-six years of our good times together, of Ivan as an infant, then young boy, teenager, college student, and finally adult, swept through my troubled mind like a cleansing breeze. And then I really couldn't stop the tears from flowing as we sat together in silence, the joy and tragedy of this moment fused along with our clasped hands.

Dr. James had been so right. How could I have doubted that having Ivan come to see me was the right thing to do? What could possibly have been in my mind? Shame, pride? Nonsense. He was my son, and after twenty-six years of my being there for him, it was now his turn to be there for me. His need to see me was as strong if not stronger as my need to see him.

"Why don't the two of you take a little walk, just to get out of this little room?" Amy suggested.

At first I shook my head. I felt glued to the bed by exhaustion. But finally I roused myself, put on my robe, and with Ivan to support me on one side, and my cane on the other, the two of us made a few circuits of the quadrangle. For so many years that had been one of our favorite activities as father and son, to take walks together, and here we were, in a time of crisis, doing so once again. I was tired, though, so very tired, and soon asked if we could return to the room. As it grew clear that I would soon be unable to fend off sleep much longer, they both left shortly thereafter.

The day after Ivan's visit I asked Dr. James to stop giving me Neurontin. It didn't seem to be helping that much, and I feared its growing side effects. The fantasy of being unable to eat or swallow kept haunting me. To my surprise, he agreed. He had a more ambitious plan in mind anyway—to send me home. His original plan to have me stay two or three days in Unit A had stretched into more than two weeks, and now, he said, the hospital environment was less a help than a hindrance.

While his news should have been encouraging, it had the opposite effect. I had come to feel safe and protected in Unit A, and I could not imagine how I could live, or how Amy could take care of me, in my present condition. But where I saw little improvement, Dr. James insisted he could see more. And home was now, he said, the place for me to be.

"I'm not well enough," I groaned.

"I think you are," Dr. James said firmly.

"Amy can't take care of me!"

"Have you asked her?" Dr. James replied.

Actually, I hadn't, but when I did, she assured me emphatically that I had no need to worry, she could indeed take care of me. Moreover, she wanted me to come home—badly. These weeks of separation had been as painful for her as they had for me.

So for the next few days, I repeated to myself over and over, through clenched teeth: "I must do it, I can do it, I will do it."

So many people in this world have to live their whole lives consumed by despair. I would never forget the faces and the stories of the people I met during my weeks in Unit A. Nor would I forget Dr. Claussen's admonition, "Don't do anything *dumb.*" For a brief time, I had considered ending my life, but fortunately had received the prompt care and attention I needed. Not everyone is so lucky.

In the Greek legend of Pandora, all the world's ills fly out of her box to afflict mankind, but for one: hope. I left Unit A still bewitched by the poisonous chemical brew that had scrambled my brain, but during my time there I had come to appreciate the power and meaning of that myth, that of all the treasures available to us as human beings, the most precious is hope.

And as I waited for the day when Amy could take me home, that is the one tangible commodity I was able to take away from the hospital that I had not brought there—the first intimations of hope.

TEN

THANKSGIVING

Lazarus lay huddled under thick blankets, wide-eyed but unresponsive. The best physicians of the region were called in to examine him. Each offered remedies, but none were successful. Finally the greatest physician of all, a wizened old man from far away, arrived and slowly entered Lazarus's chamber. After examining the patient, he withdrew a small stone from the folds of his sleeve. "Grind this into a powder," he said, "and give it in tea." "What is it?" the other physicians asked, but the old man did not answer. He just turned and left the room.

They did as he suggested, and as soon as Lazarus drank the infusion, his eyes brightened and he looked around the room. "Ah, my dear friends. How good to see you. But why are you all gathered here? It is time for my daily walk."

And all rejoiced that Lazarus had returned to them.

After I had spent more than two weeks in Unit A, Dr. James's original rationale for admitting me to the hospital—to diagnose my drug-induced crisis—had outlived its usefulness, and, he explained, the experiment to find an antidotal drug could now continue at home. But I had grown accustomed to the hospital routine and feared to leave its safety. I found it hard to imagine that in my present distraught condition I was in any shape to function at home. But Dr. James kept encouraging me to consider that option seriously. Just as he had been adamant in advising me to invite Ivan to visit, he now contended that I needed to be back with my family.

"I'm in no condition to go home," I kept saying.

"I think you can do it," was his reply.

Whenever Amy visited, this became our main topic of conversation.

"Do you think I can do it?" I would ask her.

"Yes," she would say. "I do."

"Do you think *you* can do it?" I could only imagine how much of a strain it would be on her to take care of me in my present condition.

"Of course!" was her ready reply.

What Dr. James was offering me was a different and more ancient kind of medicine—the healing potion of family.

Months before, when I was lost in a coma, my unconscious mind still recognized the power of family to rescue, to protect and heal. In one dream I lay immobile on a gurney in a dark basement, while sinister figures rolled heavy metal storage containers all around me, a dangerous dance that kept missing me by inches. But there was my son Ivan in the midst of it all, defending me by deflecting each storage container as it came barreling at me with a push of his hand or a kick. He was protecting me as when he was a boy I once protected him.

And later, as I emerged from my coma, I had a recurring hallucination that Ivan was lying next to me in the hospital bed, and I would think, If I don't make it, at least I have a wonderful son like Ivan to carry on for me. It was a long time before I grasped that in the real world there was only one bed in the room—mine. The one that Ivan occupied existed only in my mind, along with the love I felt from him and for him.

Recently, while writing this very chapter, I had lunch with Ivan, and he shared with me a reminiscence he had never before revealed. It happened, he said, in my hospital room, the day after he and Amy had visited Yvonne, just after the doctors said I might die. Amy was out of the room. Ivan was alone with me, as I lay deep in a coma, perhaps never to emerge. Yvonne had given him a crystal image of the Buddha and taught him a Buddhist healing meditation to perform with it. For a while he did that, synchronizing his breathing with mine. Then, again according to Yvonne's advice, he spoke directly to me, saying all the things that he might never have a chance to say again, how he loved and respected me, how much he appreciated my music, my Buddhist teaching, and all my gifts to him.

And as he did so (he now told me), my eyes suddenly snapped open. The doctors had said I was in the lowest stage of coma, lacking even the most primitive knee-jerk reflexes. Yet somehow I could hear and respond to his words. Even in my near-death state, the force of family, and of his presence, was powerful enough to reach me.

After a week of reassuring me that I was indeed ready and well enough to return home, on Friday, November 12, more than two weeks after I had been admitted, Dr. James announced, "This Sunday you can go home."

I swallowed convulsively. That was only two days away.

"Once you're settled," he continued, "we'll continue experimenting. I have more drugs for you to try."

Silently I repeated the mantra I had been muttering to myself day and night for the past week, "I can do it, I must do it, I will do it!" And then aloud I asked him plaintively, "Do you still think I can get better?"

"I do," Dr. James asserted. "You know I do."

The next two days went by in a blur. If anything my anxiety and my pacing increased as this risky new change loomed on the horizon. The paperback novel about the American revolution I had discovered on the day-room bookshelf, and which I had been trying to read a paragraph at a time, now lay abandoned on the floor of my room. My attention span plummeted to zero. Nevertheless, during the daily meeting of staff and patients on Saturday, I felt a momentary twinge of pride when I was able to say, "Tomorrow I'm going home."

When Sunday came, my mood was reasonably calm. When Amy arrived just after breakfast to help me pack, I was able to focus on the details of packing and folding my few clothes and checking for anything I might have left behind. For the first time in over two weeks, my activity had some direction and purpose. A little of the excitement I had felt at Kentfield the day of my homecoming returned, along with a few moments of optimistic thinking. Maybe, just maybe, this might work, I said to myself, and repeated, for the last time, "I can do it, I must do it, I will do it."

As I was signing myself out at the nursing station and bidding good-bye to the staff, David, a patient younger than Ivan with whom I had played a few games of pool and who rarely spoke unless spoken to, suddenly appeared and held out his hand to me.

"Good-bye," he said, making real eye contact with me for the first time. "Thanks for playing pool with me."

I shook his hand solemnly. "Good luck to you," I said. I knew that soon he would be leaving this place for a halfway house, a prospect that probably frightened him as much as going home frightened me.

Then, buzzed out the security door at last, Amy and I made our way through the maze of hospital halls until we finally emerged into the morning sunlight and the parking lot. We put my duffle bag into the trunk, got in the car, and drove down the freeway. Out in the full sunshine for the first time in weeks, I noticed that my sensory fog, which the Energexol had brought back with a vengeance, was still with me. I sighed resignedly as we drove up our winding, wooded street and around the bend to our house.

"Here we are," I murmured with foreboding as Amy gunned the car up our steep driveway and parked.

I got out and inched tentatively up the outside stairs, through the front door, and into my old sanctuary, just as I had many weeks before, though this time with little sense of celebration.

It wasn't until after lunch that I felt the familiar urge rising up in me.

"I'm sorry," I said to Amy, as I stood up from the kitchen table and grasped my cane. "I have to move." And while she washed the lunch dishes, I began pacing in the living room, back and forth, back and forth. That's how I spent the whole first afternoon, flopping down every so often on the couch to rest until the urge to pace overwhelmed me and I jumped up again.

By breakfast the following morning, after a restless, drugged sleep, I was certain that what I feared most about coming home was indeed true: I was far too fragile and anxious to be left alone. With the security of around-the-clock care and the ever-present hospital staff now absent, I needed Amy to be my constant companion. Yet she could not possibly be with me twenty-four hours a day. At the very least she had to shop for food. I had feared this state of affairs while still in Unit A. It was why I had resisted this homecoming so strongly.

"How can we manage?" I asked her miserably. "This is what I was afraid of."

But unbeknownst to me, she had already anticipated this problem and found a possible solution, a home nurse to come in for a few hours twice a week, so that she could do errands, go shopping, and have a little time to herself. While I was still in the hospital, she had already contacted a nursing service and made an appointment to interview a candidate.

"I don't know," I muttered doubtfully when I heard this news. The thought of being alone in the house with a stranger was unsettling to me. But since she had already shown so much forethought, I felt the least I could do was meet the candidate, who was due to visit tomorrow.

"You don't have to decide now," she assured me. "Let's meet the man, and then we can talk it over."

The next day Ernesto, the young man the nursing service had selected for us, arrived at our front door. He was muscular, well-spoken, neatly dressed and polite. After we all shook hands, Amy briefly described my illness to him, while I sat silently on the couch. He would not have to do much, she explained, just provide companionship for me for a few hours twice a week.

After she was finished, she turned to me expectantly, and I realized I would have to say something, if only to show Ernesto that at least I could talk.

So I briefly explained my painful secret. "I can't sit still. I pace back and forth all the time. It's an aftereffect of my illness, something neurological." That was as much as an explanation as I felt comfortable providing.

"That's okay," Ernesto replied. "The last client I had, his wife had just died, and I had to stop him from jumping out the window." He was confident my situation would present no problem for him.

He and Amy spoke for a few more minutes about scheduling and practical details, but I said nothing further. In fact, in the midst of their conversation I excused myself and went back upstairs. He left, Amy told me later, with her promise to let the nursing service know our decision within a day or two.

"Well, what do you think?" Amy asked me after Ernesto had left and she had come upstairs to find me.

I was lying in bed staring at the wall. "I need to think about it."

She lay down next to me while we talked it over for some time. I did my best to be receptive but finally rejected the idea. "It feels too weird," I said. "Someone I don't even know." And even though Ernesto claimed he would not be disturbed by my behavior, the thought of having him there to witness it still bothered me.

As we continued to discuss our options, I became teary-eyed, realizing that there was really only one person whom I trusted to be with me at this time of crisis—Amy—though I knew full well that such a demand was unrealistic.

So what could we do?

I realized with sudden dismay that the only way out of this predicament was for me to take the initiative and do something I was sure I could not do. "Okay," I blurted out. "Whenever you go out, I'll go with you."

This suggestion surprised Amy as much as it scared me. "Are you sure?" she asked. "Do you really think you can do that?"

I didn't know, but I said I would try. I would wait in the car while she went shopping, or pace outside whatever shop or establishment she was in until she returned. The whole idea filled me with dread, but the idea of a home nurse was even worse. Besides, in my last few days at the hospital Dr. James had counseled me that this was a time for courage. Here was my opportunity, like it or not.

We needed groceries, so the very next morning we tried my idea. As I expected, I couldn't sit still in the car for more than a few minutes. So while Amy was in the store I paced outside on the sidewalk, certain that everyone who passed must have thought I was a madman. But I managed to hold myself together until Amy emerged. Later that day she thanked me for making the effort. She had never been comfortable, she finally admitted, with the home nurse idea either. She had only pursued it for my sake.

If only I could continue this way. I wasn't so sure.

The few days' wait until our first office appointment with Dr. James seemed interminable. When I wasn't pacing or resting in bed, I tried reading, one paragraph at a time. Pace, read, rest. Pace, read, rest. Just stick to that routine, I told myself, and somehow I'll be able to get through each day. But inwardly I despaired. I was little better, it seemed to me, than when I had first entered the hospital. I yearned for the moment each day when evening came—only a few more hours until I could take a sleeping pill and lapse into the comfort of unconsciousness. But after dinner I could not even sit still long enough to watch the nature shows on television that used to calm me when I was first home from Kentfield. I would jump up after five minutes and pace the hall outside the television room, or rush into the bedroom and pull the covers over my head, then watch the show for another five minutes before jumping up again. The whole process was most discouraging. Just as in the hospital, each day was a long, tiresome ordeal.

At last the day of my appointment came. I tried to stay put in the waiting room of Dr. James's office, but after a few minutes it was clear Dr. James was running a bit late, so I went out into the parking lot to pace while Amy remained inside the waiting room. At last Amy beckoned me inside, as Dr. James emerged from his office in his shirtsleeves, wearing his trademark red tie, to greet us with a cheery smile.

"How are you doing?" he asked me casually as though inquiring about the weather, clapping his hand on my shoulder as we walked down the hall to his office.

I had plenty to tell him in reply, and as soon as Amy and I sat down, it all came pouring out. Dr. James listened patiently, even though I had to leap up several times to pace back and forth in the small office while I talked.

Then it was his turn. Since my departure from the hospital, he told us, he had been consulting not only with Dr. Castleman but with a group of neurologists at the University of California Medical School, one of the leading medical centers in the country, the place where I had received my cancer radiation therapy many years ago and where desperate cases from all over the country were sent for last-ditch, experimental procedures.

"We've all come up with a theory," he explained.

My need to pace, my agitation, together with other symptoms, he explained, all implicated a section of the brain called the extra-pyramidal structure—an area responsible for motor control, swallowing, and speech—as a likely source of the problem. Somehow, the doctors surmised, taking the Energexol at this critical time in my encephalitic healing had elevated the level of serotonin in my brain to an unacceptable level, affecting that area as well as other neurons throughout my brain—a so-called "serotonin syndrome."

If this theory were true, Dr. James continued, the doctors now recommended two drugs, either of which might reverse the symptoms and return me to normality. The first, Cogentin, was commonly used in patients with Parkinson's disease. And the second?

"Lithium," Dr. James answered.

Lithium, I knew, was normally used to treat people with manic-depressive disorder. I had a brief jolt of anxiety. Is that what was wrong with me?

210

"No, no," Dr. James reassured me. "Lithium is used to treat many different conditions. This is just one of them."

"What if neither one of the drugs work?" I asked. "What then?"

"Then," Dr. James replied, "the neurology group at the university will see you in group consultation."

For a moment I felt encouraged that my disease was sufficiently unusual for such eminent physicians to take an interest. That impulse was immediately followed by the depressing realization that if such a meeting were necessary, it would be a last resort.

During this whole exchange I had been jumping up from my chair every few minutes to pace back and forth in the small office space like a caged animal.

"I'm sorry," I apologized to Dr. James. "I can't help myself."

He waved my apology away. "Pace as much as you like."

"How can people live like this?" I said, plopping down in my chair at last. "Have you ever seen a case this bad?"

"Worse!" was Dr. James's answer.

Worse? I couldn't imagine it, though the notion that others also suffered from this bizarre condition gave me some slight comfort.

At the end of the hour Amy and I left with a prescription for Cogentin, an appointment for a few days hence, and Dr. James's promise that he would call me every day to check on my progress.

"Can Cogentin really make a dramatic difference in people like me?" was my final question.

"Sometimes," he replied.

That also meant sometimes not. Well, what choice did I have? While I waited in the car, Amy filled the prescription at a nearby pharmacy. Then we drove home.

Dr. James called as promised the next afternoon, but I had to tell him that so far the Cogentin had produced no noticeable change in my condition. In fact, my pacing in public, near the stores where Amy was inside shopping, was increasingly worrying me. Suppose someone is offended? I asked Dr. James. Suppose someone calls the police? He gently reassured me that most people would be far too concerned with their own affairs to notice, and in any case my behavior would appear far less abnormal to others than I imagined.

"Don't worry about it at all," he said. "You'll be fine. And if there is any change with the Cogentin, however slight, call me right away."

Once again, my thorough trust in this physician who had already done so much for me was strong enough to assuage my fears.

By the time I visited Dr. James again it was clear that the Cogentin was having no effect, and I was feeling quite discouraged. Though I no longer harbored the panicky, self-destructive thoughts that had landed me in the hospital in the first place, I was fast losing hope. What was to become of me? How could I keep living like this?

"Since the Cogentin didn't work, doesn't that mean that the theory about my condition is mistaken?" I asked Dr. James.

"Not at all," Dr. James replied. "We just haven't found the right drug yet."

So on to phase two, lithium.

"I'm prescribing a fairly low dose for you," Dr. James explained as he scribbled on his prescription pad. "If it's going to work at all, we should begin to see some effect at this dosage."

So for the second time I arrived home from the pharmacy with a bottle of white pills in which I had scant confidence. I took my first dose immediately, with the irrational hope that I would feel some immediate, magical transformation. But as I suspected and feared, nothing happened.

Meanwhile, my attention and anxiety were fast shifting to another concern: Thanksgiving day. This coming Thursday Ivan would be coming for our traditional holiday dinner. During his brief visits at the hospital, in the evening when I was already exhausted, I had never let him see me truly agitated, never revealed to him how severe my condition was. Then, as now, I was ashamed of letting him see his father in such a distraught condition.

On Thanksgiving he would be coming not for a brief visit but for the whole afternoon. I couldn't possibly conceal my condition from him that long, I thought, without pacing, or crying, or otherwise breaking down emotionally. How would I cope? What would he think?

"Don't worry," Amy kept telling me with a bit of impatience when I confided my worries to her. "Ivan's your son. He loves you. Whatever condition you're in, he'll accept it. Remember, there was a time when he thought you were going to die. We both did. You're far better than that today. He'll understand."

Perhaps so, but my anxiety was not assuaged. Besides, after two days the lithium seemed to be having no more effect than the Cogentin had. I was already beginning to picture the trip to the university hospital in San Francisco, the long walk from the parking garage, sitting in a waiting room, being paraded before a panel of doctors and having to answer their questions. And as good as they were, suppose they had no answers? Suppose they had nothing further to suggest? Then what? Was this the end? Was this my life for the foreseeable future? That was a thought I couldn't begin to face.

At last the dreaded day arrived—Thanksgiving. After awakening, I stayed in bed for a long time, reviewing in my mind various strategies for managing the holiday meal and Ivan's visit. Later, once I had showered and dressed and had a bit of breakfast, I took up my usual routine in the living room—pace and sit, pace and sit. Periodically I wandered into the kitchen, where Amy was now beginning to prepare the elaborate holiday meal. Watching her dress the turkey, stir the cranberry sauce, and mix the yam casserole, and smelling the holiday fragrances, I started to weep.

"We've had so many happy Thanksgivings as a family," I said, "And now . . ." I couldn't finish my thought.

Amy stopped what she was doing and came over to take me in her arms. I had never before expressed such emotions, never revealed to her how important Thanksgiving was to me. I don't think I ever realized it myself until now.

"It's all right," she murmured, as I clutched her to me. "Think of all we have to be thankful for, how much worse everything could have been. You'll be all right. This will be a real thanksgiving for all of us."

Yes, what she said was true, I had so much to be thankful for. That was probably why my tears were flowing so freely. But I still needed to put on a good face for Ivan, or so I thought, and I still didn't know how I was going to manage it.

By the time the doorbell finally rang, I had tired myself out from crying and pacing and was back upstairs under the bedcovers. But as soon as I heard the chime, momentarily forgetting my worries, I leaped up and ran downstairs. I realized how eagerly I was looking forward to seeing my son.

"Ivan!" I said, embracing him tightly. "It's so good to see you!"

"Hi, Dad!" he exclaimed. "Wow, you look great."

Did I? Perhaps to him.

We chatted for a few moments, and then, before anything happened to spoil the festive mood, I said, "Ivan, I'm feeling pretty tired today. I think I'll go back upstairs to rest until mealtime."

"That's fine," said Ivan, taking off his overcoat and settling himself on the living room couch.

I expected to curl up on the bed again, but once I got upstairs I decided instead to change into more formal clothes. I put on dress slacks, a maroon wool sweater and sport jacket, trimmed my beard, and combed my hair, I suppose in the hope that making myself outwardly more presentable might help reduce my inner turmoil. Then I waited, fully dressed, on the bed for the summons to the meal.

Finally Amy, thinking I might be asleep, knocked softly on the bedroom door. Slowly she pushed the door open and peered in. I was quite awake, hunched on the bed, my arms around my knees.

"Dinner's ready," she said.

My hands shook as I inched carefully down the stairs, one hand on the rail, the other on my cane. The moment of truth. I took my place at the head of our dining room table—the first time I had sat in that chair or eaten a meal there since before my illness. It was my customary place as the head of the family, but I didn't feel in any shape to be the head of anything. Amy reached out to me. We all clasped hands in a moment of silence, then recited the traditional Buddhist mealtime grace. At its conclusion, we all bowed, our hands pressed together, as Ivan added, "I guess we have a lot to be thankful for this year."

I managed to suppress the tears that welled up in my eyes when he said that, as I surveyed the festive meal now spread out under lit candles. Could I find it in myself to feel a moment of thankfulness, however brief? We passed around the turkey, the gravy, the stuffing and trimmings, lifted our forks, and began to eat.

As the meal progressed, and the flavors and fragrances

of the meal stimulated me, I began to relax just a little. I found to my surprise that I was able to sit still, without any urge to jump up and pace. For a while I forgot my woes and became absorbed in Ivan's description of his new computer programming job, his latest creative writing projects, and all the news of his exciting young life.

He was doing so well, so engaged, so independent, I thought. How proud I was of him, how mature he looked to me. It was as though I were seeing him after a long absence—mine, not his.

"And how about you, Dad?" he said. "How are things going?"

I stiffened my jaw and tried to remember the story line I had been rehearsing for days in preparation for this moment.

"I'm doing all right," I said carefully. "The doctor still has me trying new drugs, trying to get me over my bad drug reaction." I glanced across at Amy as I spoke, to see if she were going to add anything, but she continued eating in silence, allowing my version of events to stand without comment.

The meal went far better than I had hoped or expected, but I didn't want to push my luck. As I finished my third helping of cranberry sauce, I announced, "I'm going to go back upstairs and rest for a while." I pushed my chair back and reach for my cane. "Call me when it's time for dessert."

For the next half hour I lay upstairs in bed, listening to the muffled sound of Amy and Ivan in animated conversation downstairs, torn between my desire to join them and my fear of what might happen if I did. Several times I thought, Go, go down, just for a few minutes. It will be good for Ivan, and good for me. Once or twice I even reached for my cane and got as far as the bedroom door. But each time I decided against it and turned back.

Finally, Amy called from the bottom of the stairs that it was time for dessert, and at last I joined them at the big table once more, for pecan pie and tea and a bit more conversation.

Pecan pie, my favorite. I had two helpings.

"Delicious," I commented, as I quickly wolfed down my portions, and once again, before there was time for anything to go amiss, I retreated to the bedroom. For the rest of the afternoon that's where I stayed, under the bedclothes, listening to the murmuring of my family downstairs and cursing myself for lacking the courage to join them. This illness has made me a coward, I thought, and I cursed the illness too.

I came down only when I heard Ivan asking for his overcoat and Amy calling up to me that he was leaving.

"So, you're going now?" I said as I reached the bottom of the stairs. Suddenly I wished he would stay longer. Now, when it was too late, I felt ready to be with him.

"Yep, time to go," he said. "It was great seeing you, Dad."

"Right," I said, hugging him tightly. "Thanks for coming. I'm sorry . . ." I was sorry for so many things. But surely there would be another time. When I was better. If I were ever better.

"That's all right," he said, patting me on the back. "I understand."

And after our final good-byes, the door closed behind him and he was gone.

Now, when it was too late to change the day, I understood. Amy had been right all along. Ivan was no boy who needed protection from the truth. He was a grown man who loved me and would have graciously accepted me, however I presented myself. The problem was not Ivan, or my illness, but my own stubborn pride. What was I thinking? Ivan was family. I was his father. He was my son.

I am not myself, was the thought that helped console me. I am not at all myself. That is why I have behaved this way.

At least I had made it through the day. I breathed a giant sigh of relief as Amy and I joined in a long, gentle embrace by the front door.

I am not myself, but I will try harder.

As soon as I woke up the next morning, I knew that something had changed, and for the better. All the anxiety and discomfort of the previous day was gone. As soon as I stood up, I could feel the change in my body. For the first time in weeks, I felt no agitation, no irritability, no urge to pace. I felt almost like—I could hardly dare think it—*myself*.

I didn't want to say anything to Amy. Not yet. Perhaps it was just a momentary respite. After all that had happened, I hardly dared hope for more. I dressed and showered, continuing to monitor my internal condition for signs of returning distress, but found none.

Finally, during breakfast, I decided to speak up. "How do I look?" I finally asked Amy as we ate our cereal.

Amy cocked her head, examining my face closely. She knew me so well. Often she could sense how I was feeling better than I could. "Different."

"Different how?" I pressed her.

"Brighter," she said. "More present."

"That's right. Ever since I woke up this morning." I was still trying to adjust to this new sensation. Even the cereal tasted better.

After breakfast, when ordinarily the urge to pace would become overwhelming, I still felt calm and collected.

"Let's try something," I said to Amy. "Let's go down to the office. I need to photocopy this memo that Mary and Jalal asked me to write. I'd like to see how I do there."

So we made the five-minute drive to the office. As soon as I entered the empty suite and switched on the fluorescent lights, I could see the difference with my own eyes. No glare, no harsh brightness. Everything in the room looked wonderfully mundane and ordinary.

After briefly switching on the copying machine and making my copies, to Amy's surprise I suggested that on the way home we stop at a nearby Starbuck's for a coffee and pastry. As soon as we entered the shop I had the same reaction as at the office: no more bright, unreal faces. No more painfully loud voices. No more sensory distortion. The normal waking world, a long-lost sensation, seemed to have returned. Buoyed with new confidence after our snack, I suggested a still more challenging errand: a visit to our local bank to reinitialize the password to my ATM card, the one number that over the course of my months in the hospital I had forgotten.

As we sat down at the bank officer's desk, Amy began to explain our need, accustomed after all these months to handling such affairs, but I surprised her by interrupting and taking over the conversation myself. I followed the bank officer to the magnetic reader, inserted my bank card into the machine, and chose a new password, one I was sure not to forget.

"Thank you very much," I found myself saying brightly to the bank officer as we left.

I didn't want this welcome new episode to end. "Let's go to lunch," I said to a now delighted Amy as we returned to the car. And so we did, to a favorite Mexican eatery that we had not visited for years. Again no anxiety, no agitation, no urge to pace, just good food and, by now, real exhilaration. Could it be? Was I really, in a snap of a finger, back to normal?

It was not until we got home that I had the first intimation of an anxiety attack. But drawing on the strength of my morning's successes, I was determined not to give in to it. Suddenly I remembered that long-ago vision of healing I had described to Diane, to hike down and up our steep residential street unaided. So I went upstairs and changed into a white turtleneck and favorite leather jacket, the costume I had imagined in the vision, and then we went outside. My body was surging with adrenaline, whether from anxiety or determination or both I did not know. Amy at my side, I edged cautiously down our steep driveway, leading with my cane, and then we were off, to walk the quarter mile down to the bottom of our street and then back up again.

Before my stay in Unit A, I had tried to walk at least a half hour every day, but always on flat land. And for the time I had been in the psychiatric unit, I had gotten little exercise except for my pacing in the halls. I was weak. Still, step by step I inched down the steep, winding road—cane, right foot, left foot, cane, right foot, left foot—Amy's hand inches from my elbow to catch me if I should stumble, but I did not need her help. By the time I reached the bottom, tears were streaming down my face.

And now the return trip, a steeper climb than any I had attempted since the onset of my illness. I had to go quite slowly, resting frequently while my harsh panting slowed. It must have taken twenty minutes to climb that quarter mile, but I did it, and at last climbed those once formidable twenty steps to our front door with an enormous sense of relief and triumph.

What a day! And to cap it off, as I sat at the kitchen table sweating, drinking glass after glass of cold water, blowing my nose, and drying my tears, I announced to Amy, "Monday I'm going in to the office."

"Are you sure?"

I nodded. I was sure.

And when Dr. James called that evening for his daily

check-in, he too was surprised and delighted. Though it had not occurred to me as I'm sure it must have to him, I had now been taking the lithium for five days. It had finally taken effect, with stunning results.

Lithium carbonate is not a designer drug but a simple mineral salt, with a chemical composition no more complicated than ordinary table salt. Its medicinal value in treating manic states and brain trauma was discovered by accident decades ago, and even today its precise mechanism is not fully understood, though it is now used for Parkinson's disease, Alzheimer's, and a host of other ailments. But it had done the trick. My team of doctors had gotten it right on the third try.

On reflection, I doubt lithium was the whole answer. Just the previous day I had been petrified at the thought of maintaining a civil conversation with my own son for more than ten minutes, but I ought not to have underestimated the power of a Thanksgiving meal, of the joining together of hands in gratefulness, of the realization of the treasure I had in my family, in spite of my agitation and illness.

Family and salt, the power of love and a simple mineral. Who's to say which was the greater force?

I can say that Monday I kept my promise, and arrived at my office bright and early to recommence my work life. Amy drove me and stayed with me the one hour I was there, while I explored my long-unused computer, made a few phone calls, and met with the people who had kept my business afloat while I had been off doing the hard work of healing.

That night I was able to report to Dr. James that I had spent an hour that morning at my office, perhaps the most significant milestone in my healing since awakening from the coma. And in the following months, there was hardly a single day I did not go to that office. It became my touchstone, my symbol of return, living proof that the power of family and a simple mineral salt had brought me back from the brink of despondency to the destination I had coveted for so long: a return to normal life.

ELEVEN

PATIENCE

Now that Lazarus had recovered from his mysterious relapse, he returned to the routines of healing that he had followed before it struck. Soon he was strong enough to open his sacred scrolls and read, and soon after that, to meet for brief periods each day with his students. They marveled that the old man, whom they had once thought they had lost forever, now explicated the sacred texts as lucidly as ever, though he tired easily, and by midmorning would rise with apology and return to his bedchamber to rest.

If this book were a novel, the previous three chapters should be culminating now in some dramatic climax. But since real life does not follow the conventions of fiction, what happened after I began taking the lithium was less dramatic—a return to the slow daily healing of the weeks before the Energexol episode. But all was not as before. The lithium had restored me to normalcy, but now I had been hit with not one but two psychic earthquakes—first the encephalitis, and now the Energexol. I had to heal from these psychic aftershocks as well as from the disease itself. And that healing would not go as quickly as learning to stand or walk. For the next several months, I would have to cultivate patience.

Patience has never come easily to me. I had always counted on my quick intellect to solve life's problems—a kind of inflated Superman self-image. But in healing from this disease my mental quickness was of little use. I was faced with a problem I could not solve with my speedy brain. And brain cells heal more slowly than any other part of the body. Given the complexity of the brain, it is a miracle that it heals at all.

Buddhism considers patience one of the six virtues essential for spiritual success, but the word it uses implies something more active than sitting in a railway station waiting for a train. The Buddhist word *kshanti* means tenaciousness or perseverance, the kind we would need for a long journey on foot. Seated meditation is the classic Buddhist method for cultivating patience. The idea is to accept whatever comes into consciousness, to let that thought be, allow it to linger, and eventually pass away. I had spent years of my life engaging in this practice and, eventually, teaching it to others. After my illness, I had tried many times to return to this practice, once so central to my life, but it was only after the lithium that, for the first time, I was able to do it with some success.

The other important change that the lithium had now made possible was my return to work. Now I was going to my office every day, at first for only an hour, but soon for two or three. In my book *Work as a Spiritual Practice,* I described how important it is spiritually and emotionally for each of us to have some useful work to do. But now I had a chance to learn that lesson firsthand. Freud himself, when asked to define psychological well-being, replied, "To love and to work." Each day, when I awoke, I now had a purpose. Instead of lying in bed or on the couch all day, those two or three hours at the office gave my whole day focus and meaning, and lifted my spirits.

As the New Year turned and January began, I marveled at the miracle of my lithium cure, as well as all Dr. James had done for me. What he had said to me soon after I met him—"I'd swear in court that you'll get better"—had indeed come to pass, through his and Dr. Castleman's diagnostic skill in unraveling the mysteries of my bizarre syndrome. And it was not just Dr. James's skill that brought me back, but also his commitment and dedication. In the hospital he visited me every day, even on weekends. A trip from his home to the hospital was a forty-minute drive, and I suspect some of those weekend trips were just for me. Those visits were my lifeline. And now that the worst was over, I felt I had found more than my mental balance, but also a mentor and guide who could now help me through the complexities of the next lengthy period of healing.

And I still needed his help; I was still experiencing the same unusual symptoms as I had before the Energexol episode. Fortunately, the one symptom that had bothered me most at Unit A—the increased loss of sensation throughout my body—had dramatically subsided within ten days of starting the lithium. I had not really noticed how much better it was until Dr. James asked me about it and I could report that though my feet were still somewhat numb, as was my face and right hand, and parts of my left leg, otherwise all the improvement I had gained since the coma had been restored.

"How about the bright light and loud sounds?" Dr. James asked. "That feeling of a firecracker in your brain?"

"Gone," I replied triumphantly.

"Good!" he replied. "Those are lower-level brain functions. That means there's been a fundamental change for the better."

It was then that I began to explore with him what I called "dips," sudden alterations in mood. At these times, most often in the early morning, the world felt unreal and distant, and my emotional responses were often unusual. As I described it to Dr. James, "Even the chairs seem sad to me."

He nodded at that description and did not seem to require any further explanation. And when I added that sometimes emotionally charged phrases would pop into my head too, such as, "I can't go on," he nodded again.

"What's going on?" I asked.

"That's primary process material," he explained.

"Primary process?" I was not familiar with the term.

"Material emerging directly from your unconscious. Like the 'sad' chair. That's not coming from your conscious mind. It's more like a feeling in a dream."

"Is this still the encephalitis?" Was the disease itself still causing some part of my psyche to linger in a dream world, even during the day?

"It could be. It's hard to say," was Dr. James's reply. He went on to explain that this could be a primary after-effect of the encephalitis, or a psychological by-product of the post-traumatic stress from the disease and the Energexol episode, or both. In any case, it was now clear that there was a fissure, or rift, in my mind, through which unconscious material was leaking into my waking life.

As these "dips" or leaks continued, I experimented with ways to confront them. Early one morning, when Amy had already left for work and I was alone in the still-dim living room, I instinctively decided to give voice to these obtrusive thoughts and said aloud, "I'm afraid!"

The voice that spoke these words was hardly recognizable—deep and tremulous with fear. Yet it was clearly my voice.

"What are you afraid of?" I answered myself in my normal voice.

"I can't move," the tremulous voice replied.

"Why not?" my normal voice asked.

"I can't talk! I'm afraid! I'm afraid!"

Now I was beginning to understand. This voice was stuck in time at the moment I awakened from my coma, unable to move or talk, disoriented and terrified. That frightening moment was months ago, but it had been seared into my unconscious memory, and the terror I had felt was still buried there, still haunting me.

Dr. James confirmed my suspicions. "The unconscious has no sense of time. If your dog died twenty years ago, as far as the unconscious is concerned, it happened yesterday. Everything in the unconscious, past and present, is commingled."

"Could that be why I have so much trouble with time?" I had told Dr. James of the period before my hospitalization when time felt distorted and ominous. To some extent, particularly on weekends, that sensation still persisted.

"It could be," Dr. James agreed. "The unconscious, in its own primitive way, is always trying to protect you, but it is suspicious of anything connected to the rational mind, and that includes time. The unconscious would find the notion of time quite disturbing."

At last some of the mystery of my condition was beginning to be explained. Many months before, a good friend had remarked that I had the look of someone who had "seen another world." While in my coma, I was completely lost in that other world, a world of vision and dream, and now, months after I had awakened from it, some part of me was apparently still connected to it.

If the encephalitis or its effect on my brain chemistry had indeed opened a fissure or rift between conscious and unconscious, that would explain so much—the sensory fog, when the whole world had a lit-up, dreamlike quality; the oppressiveness of time; my difficulty concentrating— even the Energexol episode, which may have temporarily widened what was a narrow fissure into a gaping hole. Who knows what damage those tiny virus cells had wrought as they wormed their way through the delicate, complex tissue of my brain?

Meanwhile, my daily mood dips, with their voices from the unconscious, continued.

"Keep working with these states," Dr. James encouraged me. "The unconscious doesn't like the rational mind, but it is receptive to guidance from it. It can be told what to do, and it responds well to repetition, and lots of detail."

I didn't know the unconscious had such particular tastes, but the next time the "voice of terror" surfaced, I answered it in my ordinary voice, speaking calmly as though to a frightened child, "That happened many months ago. You're much better now. You don't have to be afraid anymore."

"I'm afraid," the frightened, quavering voice repeated.

"There's no need to be afraid," I repeated. "Your mind was damaged then. You were near death. You were confused. That time is in the past."

These self-dialogues continued, off and on, for a few weeks, and slowly the voice of terror began to recede. Then one day, instead of the voice of terror, a new voice suddenly appeared, speaking in the high falsetto of a very young child.

"Who's going to take care of me?" it cried plaintively. "There's no one to take care of me!"

I said the first thing that came to mind. "I'll take care of you," I replied firmly in my normal, adult voice. And then, thinking of what I would have said to Ivan when he was that age, I added, "You're safe now. Go to sleep."

And amazingly enough, after a few more days of dialogue with the child, during which I repeated my suggestion to go to sleep, it did, and I did not hear from it again.

Who was this fearful child? It was me, of course, but when? When would I have had such a fear? As I thought about it further, I gradually understood. The day before my fourth birthday, my mother had died. This child's voice was not from the recent but from the very distant past. I had no conscious memory of that time, no recollection of the terrible fear of abandonment I must have had then, but that powerful emotion was well preserved in my unconscious, and was surfacing now.

And this time, when I told Dr. James about this interchange, it opened up whole new avenues of inquiry, into long-buried ancient childhood fears of grief, loss, and abandonment that the helplessness and terror of the encephalitis had unearthed and brought back into consciousness. We continued to explore this topic in many later sessions, as I began to realize how much the trauma of the encephalitis experience was like this other, equally frightening one, from long ago.

One morning, as I sat in the living room watching the sky outside the bay window grow slowly brighter, instead of engaging my inner voices, I had a distinct image of a veil, thin and delicate like a spider web or a woman's stocking, beginning to cover the opening between conscious and unconscious worlds. And that day no voices appeared.

When I told Dr. James about this image, he leaned forward intently. "Now that's fascinating," he said. "Rorschach himself once described the barrier between conscious and unconscious as a thin screen, like a fine wire mesh."

"Does that mean that the gap is closing?" I said, excited that perhaps at last I was making some real progress.

"Perhaps. Let's watch and see what happens."

And over the next few weeks, the image of the veil grew steadily thicker. At the same time, my mood dips began to decrease in frequency. Gradually, the veil did solidify, though for quite a while, as Dr. James said, "the cement isn't dry yet."

Dr. James once commented as I was reporting my progress, "Researchers are only just now trying to find the physiological location of the unconscious in the brain."

"And you think the encephalitis damaged that part?"

Dr. James chuckled. "Well, we still don't know where it is yet. The important thing is that you're getting better."

It was only months later that Dr. James confessed that he had been more concerned about this "crack" in my mind than he let on at the time.

"I was worried about you, for a while," he confessed. "Your symptoms were quite unusual."

"What other conditions cause it to happen?" I asked.

"A high fever, psychedelic drugs, a blow to the head," he answered. "But your manifestation was unique. To tell you the truth, I've never seen it before in a person who was otherwise so normal."

Another symptom that troubled me was a tendency to worry excessively. Any unexpected disappointment or uncertainty—a surprise bill from the insurance company, a business client with an urgent problem, Amy returning home late—made me inappropriately anxious, sometimes for days. In the past I had always seen worry as something positive—a problem to be tackled and solved. But now, perhaps because of my unconscious "leakage," my worries quickly ballooned into major impediments that my rational mind was helpless to overcome.

As soon as I broached this with Dr. James, he reached for the thick sheaf of papers that was the output of my Rorschach test. Time and again the Rorschach had proved its spot-on accuracy in portraying my inner psyche, and this time was no exception.

Dr. James showed me a graph, which I could see was an inconsequential wiggle at the bottom of a chart.

"This is your score for compartmentalization, or the ability to handle worry," he said. "We call it lamda. You can see how low it is."

"It's hardly there at all," I agreed. "Why is it so low? I never used to have this problem."

Dr. James smiled. "Well, that was before you had encephalitis!"

Or before I had oil leaking out of my psychic engine block, I thought.

Then he continued, "Compartmentalization is the ability to set a thought aside and not obsess about it. All of us do it; it's a normal defense mechanism against stress. People whose ability to compartmentalize is too high appear to avert their gaze from their problems. Those whose score is low, like you, worry excessively, even when there's nothing they can do about the problem but wait."

Patience again. These days I became impatient and fretful just waiting in the grocery line.

"What can I do about it? As hard as I try, I can't stop thinking about these worries. They keep my head in a whirl all day."

"I know," Dr. James replied, "but the good news is that there is a simple, experimentally proven way to strengthen your lamda."

I was all ears.

"Pick some time in the future—later in the day, or the week, and tell yourself, 'Until I finish taking my shower, or until dinner, or until this Thursday, I won't think about my problems.' And then when the time comes, keep your promise—we call it 'promise to pay'—and spend some time, but not too much, dealing with what's worrying you."

"That's all?" I was surprised. It seemed so simple.

Dr. James nodded. "That's all. If you keep at it, like a physical exercise, you can bring your lamda up in a few weeks."

The exercise he described appealed to me. It was much like the Buddhist mindfulness practices with which I was so familiar, or like a vow, another spiritual practice that I knew well.

I couldn't wait to try it.

But I soon discovered it was harder than it sounded. Even though I would vow to put my worries aside until a later time, they kept seeping back, like rain through a leaky roof. Here was where I needed to apply patience with real energy and fortitude, although, as the weeks passed, I was able to report to Dr. James some modest improvement. I also found that when the time came to make good on my promise and return to my worries, I was often embarrassed to discover how petty and insignificant they then seemed. How could such trivial matters have been bothering me so much? That was the whole point— by providing some time for the worries to remain safely hidden in the unconscious, and not letting myself be obsessed by them, I let their power gradually seep away.

But there were some worries I could not compartmentalize, no matter how hard I tried. These had to do with my health. I had been blindsided by the Energexol incident, not to mention the original encephalitis—struck twice by lightning. Would something similar happen again? My whole nervous system was on red alert for any physical symptom that might signal another relapse.

When I brought this up with Dr. James, he turned to yet another page of my Rorschach report, this one showing a graph that rose to the very top of its chart. It looked familiar.

"Remember this from the hospital? This is your hypervigilance score," he said.

Yes, I certainly did remember.

He had explained hypervigilance to me at the hospital, but I had to confess to him now that I hadn't remembered much of what he had told me then.

"Think of a person," he said, by way of explanation, "who lies awake in bed at night listening anxiously for sounds of an intruder. That person will react to every sound, innocent or not, and is probably less likely to identify a real intruder than an ordinary person startled by a genuinely unusual noise. Hypervigilance is another way your unconscious is trying to protect you, but it is not very efficient and requires a lot of psychic energy.

"Remember, the syndrome usually starts with some 'sensitizing event,' typically a severe childhood trauma combined with a feeling of helplessness, and a sense that the adults around the child are equally helpless."

Now what he had told me earlier at the hospital made more sense to me. After my mother's death, my father had no idea how to handle his feelings, much less those of his two small children. And this was in the early 1950s, long before the days of grief and family counseling. That plaintive cry of my inner child—"Who's going to take care of me?"—implicitly acknowledged the sense I must have had then of my father's own sense of helplessness. The encephalitis was a psychic replica of that childhood experience: a sudden trauma, a feeling of complete helplessness, and my perception—this time mistaken—that all my caregivers were powerless to help me.

So now I found myself monitoring my physical condition continually. Were there any new spots of numbness today? How was my balance? My coordination? Did my writing seem any less legible? One incident in particular revealed how truly irrational my hypervigilance could be. In late January my feet started to feel strange again. Suddenly they were uncomfortable, painful, and tingling. What was happening? Was the Energexol rearing its ugly head again?

I found the sensation extremely disturbing, and experimented with a number of strategies to relieve it, from special socks and shoes to lying for long periods with my feet elevated. One day I hit upon what I thought might be an excellent solution—to rub Bengay all over the soles of my feet.

To test its effectiveness, I took a walk. My coordination and balance, still shaky at best, became worse and worse as the walk went on, until I stumbled into the house in tears, convinced that some new encephalitic relapse was on its way. Some small part of my mind correctly surmised that by numbing the soles of my feet, I had reduced my ability to sense the ground under my feet, thus affecting my balance. But my hypervigilance, in its misguided effort to protect me, was ringing every alarm bell. The physical effect of the Bengay wore off in a few hours, but it was days before my rational mind was able to regain control and I could calm down about it. Only then could Amy and I laugh a bit about what we came to call the "Bengay incident." But at the time, it was no joke.

I didn't realize it until much later, but the sensations I was feeling in my feet were actually the beginning of a return to normal nerve functioning. My feet were not getting worse, they were healing. My hypervigilance had noticed the change but did not have the rationality, perspective, or patience to correctly interpret its meaning.

Thus the spring of 2000 passed—February, March, April—with no more crises. Amy and I were now looking forward to a two-day vacation in mid-May—a kind of anniversary celebration of my illness. Week by week, physically and mentally, I was becoming stronger. My hours each day at the office were slowly becoming more productive. More and more I ventured out of the house for errands and meetings with friends.

But fate was not yet finished with me. The week before we were scheduled to go on our trip, Amy developed a bad cough and fever. She had had her yearly flu shot, and it was late in the year for flu anyway. We both assumed it was just a bad cold. That is until the morning she called me at the office with shocking news.

"I've just returned from the doctor's office," she told me. "Now try not to worry too much, but I've got pneumonia."

Panic swept through my body. Another of my worst fears realized. I rushed home and stumbled through the front door and into her arms, shaking with emotion.

"Do you have a fever?" I asked, pressing my hand to her forehead.

She nodded, her hand over her mouth, still coughing.

"How high?"

"One hundred two. But I've already started antibiotics." She embraced me again. "Don't worry. It will be fine. I'll be fine."

Don't worry! Another of my Three Terrors had just come to pass. All these months, I had come to rely on her so much. I couldn't imagine how I could function without her physical and emotional support. My brain's already overactive worry circuits were burning up. Pneumonia was dangerous. People died from it. Some cases were resistant to drugs. What would I do if she had to go to the hospital? How could I take care of her, when I could (I imagined) barely take care of myself?

Intellectually I knew I was worrying myself into a tizzy, but this crisis was far beyond my powers to compartmentalize. Instead I heard the plaintive cry of the sad little boy inside my brain—"Who will take care of me?"—along with more dreadful thoughts that I could hardly bear to imagine. How could this be? What would I do?

I followed Amy upstairs to bed, tucked her in, and

wrung out a cold washcloth for her forehead, all the while listening to her coughing, coughing. A hideous sound.

Suddenly I was the caretaker and she the invalid, sicker than I had ever seen her. Now I had to try to cook, shop, clean, keep working, and tend to myself and my own inner demons without her customary cheerful support. And every night, all night, I had to listen while she shook the bed with her coughing. I mopped her hot forehead; all the while dire thoughts swam wildly through my brain. And with those thoughts, the realization that I loved her so much, and how painful it was to see her so ill.

That week I thought of canceling my appointment with Dr. James, but I realized that if there was any time I truly needed him, it was now. As I poured out all my worst fears to him, he listened closely in his usual compassionate and patient silence. Finally he spoke. "Well, this is your test. You have to decide now whether to stay that lost little boy or be an adult again."

I nodded miserably. I knew he was right, but why, just when things were beginning to look up, did this have to happen? Why yet another test?

"I think you're strong enough," Dr. James added. "I think you can handle it." He was encouraging, but I had grave doubts.

It was trial by fire, both of Amy's fever and my burning imagination. Though her fever subsided after a few days, and it soon became clear that the antibiotic was working, her coughing persisted, day and night, and she was too weak to do more than lie in bed.

It was three weeks before she was significantly better, and it was time for her follow-up X ray. We drove to the radiation clinic and I waited anxiously in the waiting room, squirming in my chair and wringing my hands. And then back home, we waited some more for the doctor's office to call with the results.

At last, late that day, the phone rang. Amy answered, listened, and turned to me with a thumbs-up sign. "Clear," she announced, and I nearly collapsed with relief and gladness.

Over the course of those weeks I had learned, to my surprise, that Dr. James was right; I had been strong enough to handle it. The slow, patient inner work on my worries throughout the spring under Dr. James's skilled guidance had paid off. And as Amy's coughing gradually subsided and the month of June began, I knew that I had passed another critical milestone of healing—the knowledge that I could, if required, stand on my own two feet.

And so we made new reservations for that two-day trip to the beach town of Bodega Bay, which now was to become a celebration of both the anniversary of my illness and Amy's return to health.

As the months passed leading up to this happy moment, I learned patience, a virtue that I had bypassed as unnecessary for much of my life, and which I had failed to fully appreciate even after all my years of silent meditation. Day by day and week by week, nothing changed quickly. I awoke each morning with the dreary thought: Another day just like yesterday. How will I get through it?

But I had now joined the ranks of all those ill or healing individuals who follow the dictum to live one day at a time not as a philosophical credo but as an unyielding necessity. One day at a time. In Buddhist lectures, I used to call this "thick time." It's the time we experience when there is nothing we can do but just live, as well as we can. Thick time is not easy, but it is how things actually are, or, as my Buddhist teacher would say, things-as-it-is.

TWELVE

COMING HOME

Lazarus was in his studio, teaching his students the sacred texts. Suddenly he looked up from his scrolls and said, "Set aside your texts. Please listen to me. I have something I want to tell you." And slowly at first, and then with increasing eloquence, Lazarus described all that had happened to him during the course of his recovery, gradually revealing all the sorrow and joy, the fear and gratitude, that had filled his heart. The afternoon shadows were long by the time he finished, but when he finally stopped, a great silence filled the room. He closed his eyes for a moment and smiled. At last, he thought, I am healed, I have come home.

Healing is a biological, psychological, and spiritual process, a journey whose ancient secrets are stored in every cell of our body. The modern world has accustomed us to quick results in every realm, including the medical. We lack the patience for long journeys; we want all our travels to be by airplane. But a journey was different in the ancient world. In those days to travel meant to endure hardship and danger. Even today, healing is still more like the ancient than the modern journey. We may have learned to travel by airplane, but actual healing, cell by cell, still proceeds the old way.

Not all healing ends in full recovery, of course; as Dr. Doherty said to me so many months ago, I was one of the lucky ones. I think of all those broken bodies and minds I left behind at Kentfield, those who would never be whole, but would leave the hospital permanently disabled. Yet even for them, there was vindication. Charlene had already been at Kentfield eighteen months when I arrived. She was a victim of a car accident who entered the hospital so paralyzed that at first all she could do was move her eyelids. Her progress had been painfully slow, but miraculous nonetheless. I saw her many times during my stay, traveling the hallways in her electric wheelchair, waving and smiling. Once she and I were partners on a field trip. While I practiced using my walker, she worked with her

247

therapist to learn how to cross the street in her electric wheelchair. The day she was discharged was a celebration not only for her but for all the hospital staff. They all crowded around her in congratulation, as her husband stood proudly behind her wheelchair. After so many months, after so long a healing journey, she was going home.

Discharge from the hospital was not the conclusion of my healing, only the beginning of it. Because of the gradual nature of encephalitic healing, it is arbitrary to point to a time when it can be called complete. Typically, healing from serious encephalitis, as with a stroke, lasts two years. As I write this, I still have a few months before reaching the two-year mark. But I have chosen to mark the weekend of June 14, 2000, as the homecoming day of my healing—the weekend that Amy and I spent our first two nights away from home since the onset of my illness.

We planned to spend the weekend at Bodega Bay, a picturesque fishing village about an hour's drive north of San Francisco. There was a certain poignancy to our choice, for it was the very place we had been planning to go the week I fell into a coma. Two weeks before the encephalitis hit full force, when I was still home sick with a fever, we had debated whether we should cancel the reservations. I said no, insisting that I would recover soon. We hadn't had a vacation in many months. I was really looking forward to the trip.

Of course, we never made it. The weekend we had reservations at Bodega Bay, I lay in a hospital bed in a coma. But even then, I remained aware of our plans. In one coma dream I imagined us there, attending an imagined annual festival held every year at our favorite restaurant, featuring dishes made from, of all things, a cow's uterus. A symbol of rebirth? The dream's attempt at humor? I don't know.

Even after I awakened, in my semiconscious daze I still persisted in thinking that we would have to leave soon to keep our hotel reservations. It was several more days before I finally realized the truth—the day I had been so long anticipating was already two weeks in the past, and I wouldn't be going anywhere, not for a long, long time.

Almost a year had passed since then. In March 2000 we decided I was well enough to take my first trip away from home, and we made our reservations at Bodega Bay for mid-May. Although it hadn't been quite a year, we imagined this short jaunt as an anniversary celebration of my recovery. But Amy came down with pneumonia, and the trip again had to be postponed. She needed to recover from her illness, and I from my shock and worry. It was only as her lingering cough at last withered away, and my anxiety subsided, that we made new reservations for June. This time nothing would stop us. Bodega or bust!

I eagerly looked forward to the trip, which represented so much to me, but as I thought of leaving our house, which had served as such a sanctuary for me, I was also anxious about it. The successive traumas and setbacks of the past year had shocked my nervous system, which remained on high alert. So I still trod cautiously into any new situation, mentally sniffing and peering all about, to make sure that what had happened so many times before was not about to happen again.

Besides, it was still physically difficult for me to sit for extended periods, and my feet burned and tingled, especially after a period of immobility. I wasn't sure how well I would manage a long car ride.

In the few days before our departure, as I visualized us getting in the car and driving away to this distant place where I might face unpredictable new problems, I kept reciting the Buddhist compassion prayer, with myself as its object:

May I be safe.
May I be thoroughly safe.
May I have physical ease.
May I have mental ease.
May I have comfort and well-being.

Each time I said the word *safe*, I felt it percolating down through my mind like water into sand. Safe. I am safe. I will be safe. I didn't feel at all certain this would be so, but I hoped the power of the compassion prayer would help to make it true.

Of course any real safety in our lives is an illusion that we perpetuate in order to live without constant fear. Understanding that we are never truly safe, but allowing our minds to ignore the less likely dangers in our lives to maintain our peace of mind, is really just another form of the Buddha's First Noble Truth: all human existence is characterized by suffering. Those of us lucky enough not to be suffering at this moment have the luxury to let the full force of this truth subside into the shadows. Those not so lucky must face this fact full on.

At this point I was caught somewhat between those two extremes. The shock of my illness still made me overly sensitive to the possibility of danger, but not nearly so much as a few months before. I hoped that this trip would help me clear out the last cobwebs of trepidation from my healing brain.

On the day of our departure I checked and rechecked all the items essential to my well-being: my medicines, my foam pillows, my therapeutic stockings to keep my feet from swelling, and so on. I finally had decided to take my laptop, thinking that I might want to do a little computer programming or writing while I was away. Before my illness, when I frequently traveled on business, the laptop was my essential tool. I once had a checklist of all the peripheral equipment I needed for it, but after so many months I could not find it. No matter; this was no business trip, and I was sure I remembered all the essentials.

At last we locked the front door behind us, closed the trunk, and strapped ourselves into our seats. With a mixture of excitement and apprehension, I arranged my foam cushions, removed my shoes so my feet would not get too hot, and we were off. While Amy drove, I watched the familiar scenery pass by, already beginning to anticipate the familiar sights and sounds of Bodega Bay and the room we would be staying in, a favorite one Amy had specifically requested, high up on a hill overlooking the boat harbor and the bay.

We stopped for lunch in an outdoor café in the rustic town of Petaluma. I was in good spirits. The sun was shining, the crowd was carefree, the food hearty. I ordered their specialty, roast pork with barbecue sauce, and some nonalcoholic beer. My feet, which often became swollen and painful after extended sitting, were fine, and I was increasingly confident the rest of the journey would be uneventful.

Soon after leaving the restaurant and the town of Petaluma behind and entering the rolling grasslands and cow and sheep pastures of the California coastland, I fell fast asleep and did not awaken until we were just a few miles from the coast highway and the town of Bodega Bay.

After we passed the last hills and a stand of coastal pine, we could finally see the ocean, sparkling and calm on this bright, windless day. The coastal fog that often made the seashore dull and gray this time of year was a glittering white ribbon far off on the horizon. The sky was crystal clear.

While Amy registered at the front office, I waited in the car. I was already imagining a dip in the hotel's hot tub and perhaps a few laps in their spacious pool. I had not swum a stroke since my illness. I wondered if I were now strong enough to do it.

Then we drove up a steep hill to the parking lot next to our room. Ordinarily, I would be the one to load myself down with most of the bags, but in my present condition I confined myself to the lightest burdens. It took us three trips to completely unpack, until at last we were all settled in a spacious room with a vaulted ceiling, fireplace, plush couch and chairs, and a complimentary bottle of wine. It would be an expensive night's rest, but after all we had been through, we felt we deserved the luxury.

As we began to unpack, my heart sank. I discovered that I had forgotten to bring a critical piece of laptop equipment: its security cable, similar to a bicycle lock. My habit whenever I traveled was to secure the laptop to some stationary object in the hotel room. I had learned long ago, from newspaper accounts and friends' tales of woe, that laptops were a thief's prize catch, whether in an airport or hotel room. My laptop contained all the vital information of my business and its software product, and my concern for its security long preceded my illness. I had just read a newspaper article a few days before about a CEO of a major Silicon Valley company who had left his laptop unattended for a few moments on a stage in an auditorium full of people, only to find it stolen on his return, along with the precious trade secrets of his company.

"This is no good," I said to Amy, as I rummaged through the laptop case for the third time, as though the cable might reappear by magic. "I have to be able to lock my computer."

"Nobody would steal it up here," Amy ventured, but I was already feeling the hair-trigger anxiety starting to rise in my belly.

"Damn!"

Now I could think of nothing else except solving what suddenly seemed like a major obstacle. Amy waited patiently while I fretted, knowing that I wouldn't rest until I had solved the problem, and soon I thought I had. We could buy a length of chain and padlock from a hardware store, I said, and secure the laptop by wrapping it in the chain and locking it.

"Is there a hardware store here?" she asked.

That was a good question. Bodega Bay is a tiny town, little more than a row of restaurants, hotels, and beach homes strung along the coast highway, with no proper downtown or shopping district. It was only after we had gotten back in the car and made a few inquiries that we learned that the closest thing to a hardware store was a bait-and-tackle shop out on the marina.

The shop was far out on a spit of land, next to the boat landings and marine gas pumps, and one look at its shelves told me that this was no city hardware store. All the goods were designed for the serious boater or fisherman. After explaining to the proprietor what I needed, he pointed me to a cable bicycle lock. Tightly wound and packaged in plastic, it was hard to tell if it would be long enough to wrap double around the laptop, but it was all they had. We bought it and drove back to the hotel room. Sure enough, once I unraveled it and tried to wrap it around the laptop, it was too short.

"Maybe we should let it go," Amy gently suggested.

But I would have none of it. The laptop had to be

secured. That was how I had always done it, and how I would do it now. So back to the hardware store we went.

"That bicycle lock was too short," I explained to the proprietor. "Do you have any raw length of chain?"

He shrugged and took me out back where he had his spools of chain, all designed for use on boats. The smallest size was thick enough to pull a horse trailer, but I could buy as much as I wanted. That, along with a padlock, would surely do the trick.

Back at the hotel room I spent another half hour trying this way and that to wrap this huge chain around the delicate laptop like a ribbon around a Christmas present. Amy, concealing her growing frustration with this whole endeavor, even tried to help me, but it was no good.

"Forget it!" I gave up in disgust.

After a disgruntled few more minutes hunkered on the couch, I realized the solution to the problem that should have occurred to me at the beginning—keep the laptop locked in the trunk of the car or carry it with me wherever I went.

This was hardly an auspicious beginning to what was supposed to be a celebratory weekend, but after changing into our bathing suits and locking the laptop in the car trunk according to plan, we padded off to the hot tub and immersed ourselves in its hot, swirling waters, basking in the late-afternoon sunshine. My frustration with the laptop and my worries for its safety were now forgotten. This was the moment I had been looking forward to for weeks, one that brought back wonderful memories. It was just like the old days.

The next morning dawned clear and sunny. We had decided the night before that we would have breakfast at a tiny down-home café down a narrow, winding road next to the boat harbor. It was not a tourist site but a place for locals. Once again, it brought back so many memories of previous vacations and happy times. With the laptop propped securely on the chair next to me, I had the huevo rancheros, no cheese, and relished the spicy flavors on my tongue as I gazed out through the window on the rows of clanking pleasure boats and the sun-dappled bay waters beyond.

After breakfast we drove to the miles-long, nearly empty beach that fronted on the open ocean next to the entrance to the bay. To walk the length of this beach, from the park entrance to its terminus at the harbor mouth, was another recreation evocative of many previous visits. Until recently I would not have had the coordination to negotiate the uneven sands, and even now I did not have the stamina to walk more than a short distance, but I was pleased to find that I could keep my balance with little difficulty, even though once again I had the laptop slung over my shoulder. I was unwilling to leave it in the car even for this short excursion. While Amy gathered tiny seashells, I relished the open space, the clear sky, and the intimacy with the pulsing heart of nature that only a stroll along the surf can provide. I had been cloistered in the narrow confines of home and office for so many months, this excursion on such an expanse of open land, breathing air so fresh, was a cleansing medicine to a mind too long

closeted in illness. I hadn't enjoyed myself this much in—
I couldn't remember how long.

When we got back to the hotel, we were both a bit
tired, so after another dip in the hot tub we went back to
the room and rested, I on the couch and Amy on the bed.
After a while, still basking in the afterglow of our morning walk, I propped my head up on one elbow and casually asked, "So, are you having a good time?"

I was dumbstruck when she suddenly burst into tears.

"What's wrong?" I said, truly mystified.

But she just shook her head and wouldn't say.

Suddenly the notion that this weekend was to be a
return to normality and the comforts of our old, pre-illness
life burst like a soap bubble. For the first time I understood
that this trip might not turn out quite as we expected.
Amy's tears quickly subsided, and she turned on her side
to continue her nap, but on the couch I lay awake, uneasy
and troubled.

I began to reconsider my image of this trip. The last
ten months, I realized, had been too hard for one weekend to put those memories forever to rest. It was good to
be here, in this place redolent of such good times, but it
was unrealistic to think all could be the same as before.
Amy, always more emotionally intuitive than I, had sensed
it first, but now I was to beginning to understand too.
This time together could certainly still be a celebration,
but some of it would need to be bittersweet.

In any case, the moment passed, and after a light lunch
we drove up the highway. Two years before, the last time

we had visited this place, we had come across the Ren Brown art gallery, a charming clapboard structure nestled between the coast highway and the sea, which specialized in Japanese painters and printmakers. One artist in particular had caught Amy's eye on that previous trip. His drawings were detailed etchings of ropes, twisted and interwoven in complex patterns on a Mondrian-like background of colored rectangles and squares.

Though they were quite expensive, Amy had already decided that this time she would like to buy one, and we spent nearly an hour in the serene interior of the gallery as the owner helped Amy peruse all the works of the artist they currently had in their collection. I looked on, but felt it was really Amy's decision, her reward for all these months of hard work caring for me. After a time I grew tired—standing for any extended period was still difficult for me—so once I saw which print she had chosen, and assured her I approved, I retired to the car and waited there while the owner carefully wrapped her purchase and she paid for it.

We loaded our new treasure into the trunk of the car next to my laptop, which was still following us every-where, and returned to the hotel for a final dip in the hot tub before dinner. Whatever had been troubling Amy earlier seemed gone. She was thrilled with the picture, pleased that at long last we had finally had the opportu-nity to purchase it.

That evening we had dinner at Bodega Bay's most upscale restaurant, with large windows overlooking the bay, the ocean beyond, and the sun setting over the now-pink swath of distant fog. It was a memorable meal. I had a delicious and generous slab of swordfish and, even though I was supposed to avoid alcohol, a glass of white wine. Amy had blackened red snapper. The sourdough bread was fresh and tart, the wine a guilty pleasure, and the atmosphere convivial. Whether it was the wine or the prospect of returning home in the morning to the safety of house and home, I was able to relax fully and truly enjoy the evening. And on the seat next to me sat the laptop, its digital treasures safe and sound.

Once we were back home, it was a few more days before Amy and I had the time and perspective to discuss the trip. Some parts had been difficult, we agreed. She finally explained how much my obsession with the laptop's safety had upset her, particularly when I had struggled to wrap it with that enormous chain. We both understood that, contrary to our perhaps naive expectations, there was no "going back" to the way things were before. There never would be. Both of us had been permanently transformed by the experience. Its difficulties and stresses had certainly brought us closer, but there was no escaping the emotional and physical exhaustion that all those months of effort had imposed on both of us.

And as I reflected on the incident with the chain and the laptop, which at the time I passed off as a bit of a joke, I realized that its meaning was deeper. That laptop represented much more to me than trade secrets. It stood in for all that I still needed to protect, and feared to lose. Dr. James had once told me that the healing process begins with a need for safety, but as it progresses that is replaced by the need to once again begin taking risks. I was, I realized, on the cusp of that change. The trip to Bodega Bay had been a risk of a modest sort, but I still needed to protect what was precious to me with the largest chain I could find, and even that was still not enough. I had nearly healed from the physiological damage of the disease, but mentally and emotionally there was a different kind of healing left to do.

In the end, though, Amy and I both concluded that it was a good trip—worthwhile and rewarding. The painting is what finally redeemed it for us, I think. It is mounted on our living room wall today, and our mutual affection for it grows with each passing month. It portrays a double-braided circle of rope, drawn in super-realistic detail, with loose strands of straw protruding from the knot at the top. At various times it has reminded us of the Zen circles my Buddhist teacher loved to draw with brush and ink, or of the way that the fragile texture of life is woven from the delicate strands of each of its moments.

Seen from a certain angle, it also looks very much like a braided wedding ring, an interwoven marriage knot, as well as the countervailing truth that beneath that finished weave there is the frayed, unwoven straw that must always be worked on, and held together, if the knot is to hold.

Now, as I write, it has been another nine months since our trip to Bodega Bay. My healing continues, though my energy is limited. I still have to plan each day carefully so that I do not attempt too much.

And as the months pass and I continue to grow slowly stronger, my friends now exclaim when they see me, "You're back!"

Almost. But I still find myself more emotionally sensitive, and easily moved to tears. When I read in the newspaper or see a television segment about some human tragedy, I no longer have the option of distancing myself emotionally. Instead my imagination paints a vivid picture of what I read or hear, and I remember how lucky I was when mine was the tragic story, and how insignificant my pain compared to the agony of these others.

And in spite of all I now know, I still find myself yearning for safety, still searching for that chain big enough to protect all that is precious to me, even though I know there is no such chain anywhere. When I find myself doing that, I try as best I can to turn my attention instead to the beauty of each day, accepting its troubles along with its redeeming joys. It is hard, but I remind myself that twice in my life—first with cancer, and then with encephalitis—I have cheated what would once have been certain death. My days are doubly blessed, their time doubly borrowed. Instead of looking for a larger chain, I should be working to cultivate a larger heart.

Recently I had a dream. Perhaps it is fitting that a book that began with the dreams of a dying man concludes with the dream of a living one. As the dream began, I was in a suite of an expensive hotel, where the furnishings were plush, the down comforter under which I lay warm and toasty. I felt unconditionally safe.

Suddenly I leaped out of bed and, still in my pajamas, ran through richly carpeted hallway, down the stairs, through the ornate lobby, and out into the night, where a crowd of sinister people milled about on the sidewalk. There were no streetlamps; the air was dark and cold.

I found myself at the foot of a rope ladder, stretching high up out of sight against the outer wall of the hotel. I was afraid, but I knew I had to climb the ladder. Swinging dangerously in the wind, not daring to look either up or down, I concentrated fiercely on climbing the ladder, rung by rung, hand by hand, foot by foot.

At last I reached the top, and saw I had arrived at a narrow railed balcony. And the rope itself, I realized, was precariously secured only by one tiny metal hook. I could fall at any time. To survive I would have to swing my leg over the railing and climb onto the ledge, but the prospect of that maneuver was too frightening. I awoke.

Dr. James, whom I still see on occasion, helped me understand the traditional psychological interpretation of this dream. A dwelling, he explained, whether it be a house, a palace, an igloo, or a hotel, is a universal dream symbol for the physical body. The top of the dwelling—the attic, the roof, or in this dream, the ledge—represents the head, the brain. I was proactive in the dream, even courageous, to leave the safety of the warm hotel for the dangerous sidewalk and rope ladder—the ladder of my healing, which I was still climbing with determination and vigor. But at the top of the ladder, in my brain, something was still not quite right. Though near the end of my healing, there was something more to do.

I was satisfied with that interpretation. It seemed intuitively right to me. But for the purposes of this book, I would like to offer another understanding, more philosophical or spiritual in nature.

Climbing that ladder could also represent the Great Journey of human life itself, an expedition with no final domain of comfort and safety. If we are to find peace of mind and happiness in our lives, we must do so while in the act of climbing the ladder. Or in the words of the Buddha, "Human life is characterized by suffering, but there is liberation from suffering." We must keep climbing, rung by rung, day by day, meeting each unexpected challenge with acceptance and gratitude. That is the only way.

True safety does not mean reaching the top of the ladder, for in truth there is no top, but accepting the ladder itself as a blessing, the gift of life itself, and embracing it as our only home.

To all those who have made the long journey of healing, or who have cared for someone who has, I hope this book has been both illuminating and helpful. I have tried to report my experience as well and accurately as I can remember, and paint a picture that is neither too dark nor too light. My healing experience was inevitably colored by my personal history, my previous wounds and victories. Someone else in my situation would undoubtedly have had a different story to tell. To say that the whole experience was deeply humbling is true, but not the whole truth. It was also inspiring.

Once Dr. James asked me, "If you could magically erase this whole experience from your life and go back to the way you were before, would you?"

His challenge brought me up short. I knew that taken literally, the question was meaningless. What had happened had happened. There was no going back. But there was a purpose behind his question. Did I truly appreciate the fullness of what had happened to me, its joys as well as its terrors?

When I heard myself answer, "No," my intellect feebly protested that this was the wrong answer. Yes! It whined, I wish it had never happened. But I knew that in this instance my intellect was not to be trusted. My heart knew the right answer, and had already spoken it without hesitation.

No, I would not want to go back. This is the only life I have, and this illness has been part of it. As it says in a story of legend, life is like a tapestry, and a man cannot say, Give me only the white threads, but keep the dark ones, because I do not like them, they are evil. The tapestry exists at all only because every thread within it serves a purpose, and each one contributes in the end to its beauty.

Thus, my final message to all those who have trod the

path of healing, or are still on it, or will one day commence it:

May you be free from danger.
May you have physical happiness.
May you have mental happiness.
May you have ease and comfort in all your days.